Catechesis Revisited

Catechesis Revisited

Handing on Faith Today

LIAM KELLY

Paulist Press
New York/Mahwah, New Jersey

Published by arrangement with
Darton, Longman and Todd Ltd
1 Spencer Court
140–142 Wandsworth High Street
London SW18 4JJ

Published for North America by
Paulist Press
997 Macarthur Boulevard
Mahwah, New Jersey 07430

www.paulistpress.com

ISBN 0-8091-3997-9

Cover design by Leigh Hurlock

Phototypeset by Intype London Ltd
Printed and bound in Great Britain by
Page Bros, Norwich, Norfolk

This book is dedicated to
Mum, Dad and Basil,
my teachers in the faith.

Contents

Contents

Acknowledgements

Fr Jim Gallagher SDB first introduced me to the world of catechetics. I am grateful for his inspiration, in thought and word, for this text.

All biblical quotations are taken from *The Jerusalem Bible (Standard Edition)*, published and copyright 1966, 1967 and 1968 by Darton, Longman and Todd Ltd and Doubleday & Co. Inc.

Quotations from the documents of the Second Vatican Council are taken from *Vatican Council II – Constitutions, Decrees, Declarations*, General Editor Austin Flannery OP, published jointly by Costello Publishing Company, Inc., New York and Dominican Publications, Dublin, 1996, by kind permission of Austin Flannery OP, Dominican Publications, Dublin.

Quotations from *General Catechetical Directory and Catechesis in our Time* are taken from *Vatican Council II – More Post Conciliar Documents*, General Editor Austin Flannery OP, published jointly by Costello Publishing Company, Inc., New York and Dominican Publications, Dublin, 1998, by kind permission of Austin Flannery OP, Dominican Publications, Dublin.

Quotations from *On Evangelization in the Modern World* are taken from *The Catechetical Documents – A Parish Resource*, Liturgy Training Publications, Chicago, 1996.

Quotations from the International Council for Catechesis, *Adult Catechesis in the Christian Community – Some Basic Principles and Guidelines*, St Paul's (formerly St Paul Publications), UK, 1990. *Catechism of the Catholic Church*, Geoffrey Chapman, a Cassell imprint, London, 1994; Congregation for the Clergy, *General Directory for Catechesis*, Catholic Truth Society, London, 1997; excerpts from the English translation of *Rite of Christian Initiation of Adults*, copyright 1985, International Committee of English in the Liturgy, Inc. (ICEL) all rights reserved; and

Dominic F. Ashkar, *Road to Emmaus – A New Model for Catechesis*, Resource Publications, Inc., San Jose, CA, 1993.

Introduction

1. **Who made you?**
   God made me.
2. **Why did God make you?**
   God made me to know him, love him and serve him in this world, and to be happy with him for ever in the next.

The opening questions from *A Catechism of Christian Doctrine* may be familiar to some people. For many years, this successor to what was popularly known as the 'Penny Catechism' was the chief tool in handing on faith. This 72-page booklet, which, of course, now costs a lot more than one penny, contained everything you needed to know about the Christian faith and could be found in many homes and classrooms where 'the Faith' was taught.

The influence of this booklet can still be seen. Just a year after the death of Princess Diana, *The Times* newspaper revealed that she had been 'swotting up on the ways of Rome'. The proof? ' . . . a penny catechism, the redoubt of orthodox Catholic teaching, was found among her belongings when her apartments at Kensington Palace were cleared out'. And if you were in any doubt about what this might mean, *The Times* explained it all: 'The little red booklet contains questions and answers on the faith, such as "Who made me? God made me" . . . the doctrinal tract, which sends shivers through liberal adherents, is usually carried only by sincere believers'. So here we have a booklet which 'sends shivers' through so-called 'liberals' but is carried around by 'sincere believers'. Surely one small document, a 'penny catechism', cannot cause the division which *The Times*' article seemed to imply?

The modern definition of 'catechism' is basically a textbook of faith and morals, a manual of Christian doctrine. But the word itself is closely allied to another word which is perhaps one of the 'in' words in religious education circles today: 'catechesis'. Many parishes may well have groups 'doing catechesis', or will have 'catechists' trained to prepare children and/or adults for the sacraments. In many Catholic parishes, a group of catechists will have worked for some months with the candidates to prepare them for the celebration of the sacraments. At many confirmation ceremonies, the bishop might present a gift to each catechist, thanking him or her for the work done in preparation for the celebration. And that might be the last time the catechist is seen or heard, as the bishop then goes on to confirm those who have been painstakingly prepared for this special moment. With confirmation done, the task is over. Or is it?

A number of years ago one bishop suggested that at confirmation a present should also be given to the candidates themselves. And the ideal gift, he thought, would be the new *Catechism of the Catholic Church*, published in 1992. Its publication provoked various reactions throughout the English-speaking world (although the English translation did not appear until 1994). *The Independent* newspaper bore the headline 'Modern Catechism adds to catalogue of sins', saying that the 'comprehensive redefinition of faith and religious teaching' added 'tax evasion, drunken or dangerous driving and drug-trafficking to the modern catalogue of sins'. My own favourite story about the *Catechism of the Catholic Church* concerns the length of the text. The booklet referred to earlier, *A Catechism of Christian Doctrine*, published originally in 1898, contained seventy-two pages, summing up in memorable question-and-answer format what Catholics were meant to believe; a 1985 booklet, *The Teaching of the Catholic Church – A New Catechism of Christian Doctrine*, offered just under fifty pages aimed at those who might be interested in the Church; and the 1994 English translation of the *Catechism of the Catholic Church* was almost 700 pages in length and was addressed principally to bishops! So, seventy-two pages for everyone, fifty for enquirers, and nearly 700 for bishops! As one commentator wryly observed, 'Have they a problem which we the faithful and intelligent enquirers have not? Do they really need 1200 per cent more help?'

Of course, that was not the suggestion. But the increasing number of documents on catechesis, the trend to produce local catechisms, and the thrust in dioceses and parishes to train catechists are clear indicators that this is a key area of the Church's work in handing on faith today.

So just what is catechesis and its connection with catechists and catechisms? Is it a central feature of the Church today or just another example of religious jargon?

How This Book Might Be Used

In arguing against the practice of infant baptism Tertullian, an African Christian born in the second century, wrote: 'People are not born Christians, they become them.' At the baptism ceremony, the godparents are asked if they are willing to help the parents in their duty as Christian parents. Of course, the response comes loud and clear: 'We are.' A priest-friend of mine has been known to insert an extra question at this point: 'How?'

Although not liturgically correct, such a question can cause quite a stir. For baptism is not a guarantee of a person growing into a mature Christian, and parents and godparents make certain promises to help nurture faith. Faith is not handed on in an abstract, lifeless way as if it were some package to be hidden away, not to be opened until eternal life. It is a gift to be treasured, that it may flourish.

Catechesis has an essential role to play in handing on faith. It would be wrong to see catechesis as a modern invention of the Church, a piece of religious jargon, for it has been and always will be the Church's task to proclaim the Good News. This was the mandate from Jesus himself.

Catechesis Revisited aims to look at how faith has been handed on down the centuries. This book is not an attempt to provide a definitive commentary on the many documents the Church has published on catechesis. Naturally it is selective. In all those documents there is a richness which can only be truly experienced in a thorough reading of the original texts. This book is not a replacement but will give a flavour of what is contained therein, encouraging the reader to investigate further.

However, this is not just a history book. Looking at the history of catechesis automatically prompts the question: 'But what about handing on faith in the parish community today?' And so, in the light of that history, this book offers a model for catechesis and some pastoral, practical reflections to aid the ministry of catechesis.

This book is aimed, then, at anyone who wishes to reflect on catechesis today. It will be very useful to those who may have just been asked to be a catechist by other catechists or by their parish priest. The immediate reaction could be, 'Why me?' and this book will help to answer that question. It will also be useful for priests and for those who already work as catechists, providing a refreshing look at this important ministry of the Word. The book can be used by groups or individuals and the reflection questions adapted to suit any needs. Like catechesis itself, this book should be a point of departure.

If there were a first concern that I have about Catholic catechesis
   today
it is that we need to emphasize the joy, enthusiasm, the
   hopefulness
that confirms our own confidence in our religious heritage.
We need to speak a word that will rouse the people
who come to the church seeking not only truth, but life-giving
   truth.
In its public portrayal, religion has too frequently become a
   somber activity.
Faith has managed to be usurped by the same dour evening news
that regularly contributes to our common weariness,
as an activity rife with conflicts and controversy.
Obviously there are serious matters that involve religion.
Equally important there are the moral concerns that stem
from our religious convictions that confront societal norms and
   attitudes.
But the conflicts that are part and parcel of religious
   news
are not the heart of the message of faith.
We are people with something good to proclaim.
We are people with some good news to offer to the world in
   which we live.
The Gospel is so named because the authors and first hearers of
   the word

*were convinced that its contents, in spite of the conflicts
and suffering found throughout the Gospel,
were life-giving events for the world to hear.*

(Bishop Wilton Gregory of Belleville, Illinois, USA,
addressing National Conference of Catechetical Leadership,
quoted in *Origins*, 9 May 1996)

Part One –

Handing on Faith Down the Centuries: The Story and the Challenge

I remember every Thursday as a young child in primary school. We had to line up in twos and, come rain or shine, walk to church for Mass. Teachers were at the head of the procession as it wound its snake-like path to a big, cold church. We stopped outside to listen to our teacher. She would remind us that we were now going into 'God's house' and that required special behaviour. So, no talking, no laughing, no smirking or smiling, keep your hands joined, and don't forget to bless yourself on the way in. Another teacher was stationed next to the little bowl of water (only later did we learn the technical terms for these religious artefacts) to make sure we did it properly. 'Call that a blessing, Smith?' The admonition would be delivered in hushed tones. 'Go back and do it again.'

Then we filed into the benches, class by class. Not being too tall, I could only peer over the ledge of the bench, or just about rest my chin on it. 'I don't think it's for that, Kelly.' I remember another time talking to someone during an important part of the Mass as we were all kneeling down. Teacher tapped me gently on the shoulder and said, 'Sshh. Jesus is watching.'

I looked up and saw a man who was a lot older than me. He didn't have much hair and was wearing a funny-shaped cloth with green patterns on it. He was a long way off, through some gates and up some steps. 'So, that's Jesus,' I thought.

I was looking with the wondrous and inquisitive eyes of a child at a very complex religious celebration – the Mass. It was very much an 'adult' event, with hard words that I didn't understand, and complicated gestures and movements. However, what mattered was that I was there with my class from the Catholic primary school. And the school was one of the key partners responsible for the task of 'handing on faith'.

But before school there was the family. Every night, at home, we prayed that very popular Catholic prayer, the Rosary, five 'decades' each consisting of ten Hail Marys. This was a family event. The TV was turned off ('Oh, can't I just watch another five minutes?') and we all knelt with our rosary beads knotted round our fingers. Mum and Dad would lead us in prayer . . . and this is where it got tricky. Of the five decades, Mum and Dad would lead the ten 'Hail Marys' during the first two. That meant three more between six of us. I'm not quite sure what it did for the good of the soul, but there was much kicking and muttering 'It's your turn' during those first two decades!

So there were two very formative examples of 'handing on faith': the home and the school. Both were religious environments, where I was taught about what it meant to be a Catholic. I learned what Catholics did, what they believed (although I don't think I understood it all), what 'practising your faith' meant. The school, especially, was the primary guardian and tutor of the Catholic faith. Indeed, in the nineteenth century building Catholic schools in England was seen as more important than building parish churches. This was emphasized in the United States as well when the Bishops at the First (1852) and Third (1884) Plenary Councils of Baltimore urged the building of parish schools. Cardinal Henry Manning, Archbishop of Westminster from 1865–92, publicly stated that he considered the education of Catholic children more important than the building of a cathedral. And it goes without saying that home and school are still very important today.

For those who may have forgotten or never experienced education or handing on faith 'catechism-style' a vivid impression was given in a recent theatrical revival described in one review as a 'one-nun lesson in Christian doctrine'. *Late Nite Catechism*, written in 1992, stars a 'benignly tyrannical sister, treating audiences as recalcitrant churchgoers who are a few Hail Marys short of redemption'. It is basically an adult education class in Catholic teaching, with 'Sister' asking precise questions of the audience and chastising them for wrong answers or misbehaving in class (banishing one theatregoer to a 'penitential seat' at the side of the stage and telling off a girl for the shortness of her skirt!). The stage was a square-shaped Catholic classroom.

Although there were no 'pupils' on stage it was reminiscent of the classrooms where orderly pupils sat in front of the teacher who taught doctrine gleaned from the necessary doctrinal texts (catechisms). This content had to be memorised and the answers to the questions were for many years the heart of 'instruction' in the faith. The handing on of faith had a strong emphasis on knowledge of the Church's doctrines. Such a scene clearly fulfilled the old saying 'Faith is taught, not caught'.

REFLECTION

- What are your earliest religious memories? What do they mean to you?
- Think back to some of the religious practices of your childhood. What did they mean to you? What do they mean to you now?
- In your childhood years, who had a great influence on you in handing on faith? How?
- What do you think of *Late Nite Catechism*? Do you think it's right to treat this matter in such a light-hearted way? What message might it give? What are the advantages and disadvantages of the method it uses, the successes and failures of the era it harks back to? Does the style it revives bring back any memories?
- Where does your faith come from?

1 *Converts to Christianity*

There is an American poster which depicts six people carrying a coffin. The caption is simple: 'Will it take six strong men to bring you back into the church?' It is one of many posters designed to help the mission of churches across the United States. This particular one goes on to say: 'Our church welcomes you no matter what condition you're in, but we'd really prefer to see you breathing. Come join us in the love, worship and fellowship of Jesus Christ this Sunday.' Another advert, aimed at young adults, has a traditional image of Jesus, right hand raised in blessing: 'We don't care what you wear to church,' it says. 'And considering he walked around in a sheet, Jesus probably won't either.' The small print declares: 'Not everyone likes to dress up for church. And that's fine by us. After all, it's not your wardrobe we're interested in seeing. It's you.'

In England, a group called 'Churches' Advertising Network' ran a campaign for Easter 1999 giving Jesus a 'revolutionary new image'. The poster was very similar to the red and black 1960s' Che Guevara poster, replacing Guevara's beret with a crown of thorns. 'Meek, Mild. As If. Discover the real Jesus. Church. April 4,' the poster declared. 'We want to get away from the wimpy Nordic figure in a white nightie,' said one of the creators of this poster campaign.

Often these adverts are targeted at those people who don't go to church. The blatant aim seems to be to get them to go into the nearest church. But what happens next? How are they meant to 'discover the real Jesus'? What if they can't find him? Are adverts and poster campaigns the real means for handing on faith today? Or do they suggest faith is just another commodity in the market-place?

Of course it could be said that using posters is simply trying to communicate a religious message through modern means. 'We do not want to produce wallpaper,' said a member of the Churches' Advertising Network. 'We want advertisements that will stand up and be noticed.'

So is faith about standing up and being noticed?

Discovering the real Jesus in the early Church

In the time immediately after the death and resurrection of Jesus, his message was handed on by word of mouth. The descent of the Holy Spirit on the apostles at Pentecost gave them the courage to go and spread the message of Jesus. Peter spoke about Jesus and we read in the Acts of the Apostles of the first conversions:

> 'What must we do, brothers?' 'You must repent,' Peter answered 'and every one of you must be baptised in the name of Jesus Christ for the forgiveness of your sins, and you will receive the gift of the Holy Spirit. The promise that was made is for you and your children, and for all those who are far away, for all those whom the Lord our God will call to himself.' He spoke to them for a long time using many arguments, and he urged them, 'Save yourselves from this perverse generation'. They were convinced by his arguments, and they accepted what he said and were baptised. That very day about three thousand were added to their number. (2:37–41)

The work of proclaiming the message continued:

> These remained faithful to the teaching of the apostles, to the brotherhood, to the breaking of the bread and to the prayers.
>
> The many miracles and signs worked through the apostles made a deep impression on everyone.
>
> The faithful all lived together and owned everything in common; they sold their goods and possessions and shared out the proceeds among themselves according to what each one needed.
>
> They went as a body to the Temple every day but met

in their houses for the breaking of bread; they shared their food gladly and generously; they praised God and were looked up to by everyone. Day by day the Lord added to their community those destined to be saved. (Acts 2:42–7)

The 'teaching of the apostles' mentioned at the start of this last passage is almost a technical term for the instructions for the newly converted in which the Scriptures were explained. Here we have a very basic notion of handing on faith, a primitive catechesis which is based on the Scriptures. It is in the writings of St Luke and St Paul that we first discover the specifically Christian notion of catechesis as something closely linked to apostolic activity. Luke addressed his Gospel to Theophilus so that he might 'learn how well founded the teaching [*katechethes*] is that you have received' (Luke 1:4). In the Acts of the Apostles, Luke describes Apollos as someone who had 'been given instruction [*katechumenos*] in the Way of the Lord' (Acts 18:25). Paul speaks of those who are 'taught the word', calling the one instructed *katechoumenos* and the teacher *katechounti* (Galatians 6:6). More evidence of the scriptural basis of the teaching is given by Apollos himself, who, after further instruction from Priscilla and Aquila, went to Achaia where he was able to 'help the believers considerably by the energetic way he refuted the Jews in public and demonstrated from the scriptures that Jesus was the Christ' (Acts 18:27–8). For Luke and Paul, *katechethes* meant being taught about Christ. The word was applied both to the message taught and the oral manner of teaching.

It is important to see here the origin of the word 'catechesis'. The Greek word used by Luke and Paul comes in fact from two other Greek words, *kata*, meaning 'down', and *echein*, meaning 'to sound'. Today, we would say to re-sound or re-echo. Catechesis is handing on a message that will resound, re-echo in daily life. It is the process of echoing God's Word.

REFLECTION

• Early catechesis was very much based on the 'story of Jesus', the oral tradition and then the written Gospels. How much do the Gospels mean to you today? Are they just stories from long ago that you listen to occasionally, or do they really mean something today?

- Think of your favourite Gospel passage. How would you describe its message today?
- Apollos 'demonstrated from the scriptures that Jesus was the Christ' (Acts 18:27–8). This was his public proclamation of what he believed. If you were asked to do the same today, how would you feel? What would you do?
- From the examples in the early Church, what are your first impressions of what 'catechesis' involves?

Becoming a Christian – a way of life

I remember nothing about my baptism, since I was only a baby at the time. But in the early Church this would not have been the case. As we have seen, the preaching of the apostles and people like Apollos was directed to adults who then became Christians. With the passage of time this process received a much more formal structure while remaining firmly rooted in the message of the Bible.

One of the most ancient catechetical sources is a short Christian manual known as the *Didache*, or *The Teaching of the Twelve Apostles*. It is believed to date back to the first century and contains teaching about Christian morality, liturgy, the Sermon on the Mount, the Ten Commandments and the Lord's Prayer.

The *Didache* provides some insight into the earliest forms of catechesis. At the outset, this was still an individual process, but gradually people were prepared in groups. Within a short space of time, 'catechesis' referred almost exclusively to the instruction given in sessions before baptism. This period of formal preparation for entrance into the Church became known as the 'catechumenate', with those preparing for baptism, called 'catechumens', forming a distinctive group in the Church. Although there was no determined length of time for such instruction, it was common for it to last a number of years. Usually, a candidate was recommended to the bishop. This was because it was deemed important to verify that someone who wanted to become a Christian would be prepared to undertake the sacrifices that this might entail. This could include a change of lifestyle, since some professions – such as soldier, gladiator, prostitute – were considered inappropriate for a Christian. The community was keen to test the seriousness of those who were interested in becoming Christians and so candidates had to find a 'sponsor' who would present them for baptism after this first period of preparation. The sponsor also had to make sure that there was little chance of apostasy (a Christian's public denial of Christ) from a candidate. The role of the sponsor was thus one of guaranteeing the reliability of a candidate and a witness to their lifestyle. After providing sufficient evidence of their sincerity to become a Christian, an adult was inducted into the catechumenate in a special rite during Mass. This induction included the sign of the cross on the forehead, salt placed on the tongue, the imposition of hands, and breathing on the forehead of the candidate.

The instruction, the doctrinal preparation of the catechumens, as they were now called, took place for the most part during Mass (the catechumens were dismissed at the end of the homily, since they could not receive the Body of Christ later on in Mass). This meant that the teachers were the bishops and priests. Some saw their task as apologetic, justifying the faith against various contrary beliefs and opinions. Others saw their task as encouraging their people to lead good lives. Documents dating back to this time of the second and third centuries reflect these differences, with some having a clear moral emphasis, some doctrinal, and others more scriptural. In summary, the teaching took place within the liturgy, the teaching method was preaching, and the content was a mixture of the doctrinal and the moral. The basis for the doctrinal instruction was the Creed while for the moral it was the commandments.

A detailed account of this process of instruction in the faith can be found in St Augustine's *De Catechizandis Rudibus*, dating from about the year 400. The word *rudis* ('beginner') means simply someone who has not been taught about Christianity, and this is an important point, for Augustine's work is perhaps one of the first to acknowledge the need to take into account the different learning abilities of the listeners. Augustine writes about various teaching devices and the motivation of the cat- echumens, and, interestingly, suggests that questions should not be used as a method of teaching, but should be asked to check how much they have understood. The catechesis offered by Augustine is very much based on the Bible, a text which he believed all Christians needed to be familiar with, since it was central to Christian worship.

Catechumens who wished to continue with their instruction were encouraged to hand in their names at the start of Lent. They then became *competentes* ('co-petitioners', since they were asking for and aspiring to receive the sacraments of initiation) or *electi* ('the elect') as they took a step closer to baptism. Each day during Lent they were given instruction about the Eucharist and were bound by a strict observance of the liturgical season: wine, meat, baths, public entertainment and sexual intercourse were all forbidden. On some of the Sundays in Lent, 'scrutinies', or examinations, would take place to assess a candidate's suit- ability. These also included a number of exorcisms, vivid reminders of the chasing away of sin. Hands were imposed on the candidates and prayers chanted rebuking the devil and invoking the power of Christ. The final act of the rite was the powerful 'exsufflation', when the *competentes* were grabbed by the exorcist who hissed in their faces. The combination of the rigours of Lent and detailed instruction meant that this was a time of severe testing for the *competentes*.

As the time for baptism approached, the instruction intensi- fied and fifteen days before Easter the bishop preached to the *competentes* about the 'symbol of faith', the Creed. The candi- dates had to memorise the Creed and repeat it to the bishop, and then practise that recitation with their sponsors. All this led up to a celebration on the Saturday before Easter (the day before what we call Palm Sunday), when the whole community gathered for a vigil which included a 'scrutiny', the renunci- ation of the devil, and concluded with the recitation of the Creed on Sunday morning. The 'scrutiny' at this vigil celebra- tion was not just assessing how much the catechumen understood. It also included a physical examination to see if the *competente* had any disease that might disqualify him or her from baptism. Diseases such as leprosy or venereal disease were seen as marks of sinfulness, therefore revealing the presence of the devil. Rejection at this late stage in the process of instruction was still possible, for preparation to be welcomed into the Church was a very thorough intellectual, spiritual and physical process.

By now the *competentes* were familiar with one 'symbol of faith', the Creed, which had been recited and preached about at the celebration concluding on Sunday morning. Later that afternoon the *competentes* were given another 'symbol of faith', the Our Father, which they would recite for the first time at the Easter Vigil. Once again, the teaching about the Our Father was given in a homily which went through the prayer in great detail. In what was then called the 'Great Week', attention from Wednesday onwards focused on the liturgical celebrations. The Lenten discipline was relaxed somewhat on Thursday, when bathing was permitted and a special meal was held in the evening along with the celebration of the Eucharist (including the washing of feet). Friday was naturally devoted to the Passion of Our Lord and the whole community was encouraged to fast in solidarity with the *competentes* (the original Lenten fast lasted two days but had been extended to forty in many places by the fourth century).

The *competentes* were welcomed into the Church at the Easter Vigil which lasted from sunset on Saturday to cock-crow on Easter Sunday morning. The lengthy rite began with the lighting of the paschal candle at sunset and consisted of readings, homilies, prayers and the celebration of the Eucharist. Once again, those to be baptised recited the Creed, the symbol of faith, and baptism was celebrated immediately after cock-crow, at the dawn of a new day. First of all the baptismal water was blessed and then those to be baptised processed to the font. Once there, they removed the penitential garments they had been wearing during Lent, stood in the waist-high water and were immersed three times, professing their faith in Father, Son and Holy Spirit.

They were newly baptised into the life of Christ and his Church. Immediately the bishop imposed his hands upon them, anointed their heads with the oil of chrism and traced the sign of the cross on their foreheads. They dressed in white garments (hence the week following Easter became a 'week in white garments', garments of the newly-baptised, concluding with *dominica in albis*, the last day in white garments, which we now term 'Low Sunday' or the Second Sunday of Easter in the United States) and celebrated the Eucharist with the whole community for the first time. At the Easter Vigil, the candidates received the sacraments of baptism, confirmation and Eucharist. They were fully initiated into the Christian community, thereby breaking with the past and beginning a new life.[1]

REFLECTION

- In the early Church it was common for instruction to last two or three years. What do you think are the advantages of such a lengthy process? Can you think of any disadvantages?
- Becoming a Christian was seen as a public statement which could include a change of lifestyle. Some professions were inappropriate for Christians. How important do you think this is today?
- Do the Creed and the Our Father mean anything to you as 'symbols of faith' or are they just words? What is a 'symbol of faith'?

Instruction continues

As we have seen, instruction of those to be baptised was achieved through preaching. But what was the content of those sermons? Some hints can be gained from a look at the work of Irenaeus, Bishop of Lyons, towards the end of the second century. Using Scripture, he saw the Old Testament as foreshadowing Christ and offering 'types' of him in many of the Old Testament characters. He quotes the Old Testament and shows its fulfilment in Christ. This 'typology' was to become a very popular form of catechesis.

A clear example can be found in the writings of St Zeno, fourth-century Bishop of Verona. In a sermon on the Book of

Job, he describes Job as a 'type of Christ' and sets out a number of comparisons to show this:

> God himself called Job a righteous man. And God is righteousness itself, the source whence all who are blessed drink . . . Job was a rich man. But what is richer than the Lord? . . . The devil tempted Job three times. In the same way, as the evangelist tells us, he tried to tempt the Lord. Job lost everything he owned. And the Lord left behind his heavenly goods for love of us and made himself poor that he might make us rich . . . Job's wife urged him to sin. And the synagogue did its best to make the Lord follow the corrupt observances of their elders. It is told that Job's friends insulted him. So, too, did his priests and worshippers insult the Lord. Job sat upon a dunghill full of worms. The Lord also moved about on the real dunghill of the filth of this world amidst men seething with all manner of vices and lusts, which are the real worms . . . Job begat new sons to replace those he had lost. The Lord too begat holy sons, the apostles, in place of the prophets. Job, blessed, rested in peace. But the Lord remains blessed for ever before all ages, from all ages and throughout all ages.

'Typology' was, then, a simple tool for teaching the faith whereby the figures and events of the Old Testament were seen as foreshadowing the Christian era from the New Testament onwards.

By the time of Bishop Zeno of Verona, the term 'catechesis' had become a specific term for the instruction given in the catechumenate. This took the form of baptismal catechesis for those preparing for baptism, or mystagogical catechesis for those who had recently been baptised and whose instruction continued. This period of instruction after baptism became known as 'mystagogia' (from the Greek words *mystes*, an initiate, and *agein*, to lead).

Another example of instruction for catechumens can be found in the writings of St Cyril, Bishop of Jerusalem from about 349 until his death in 387. His *Instruction for Those about to be Illumined* is a series of talks to the *competentes*, or *electi*, during Lent and Easter.

St Cyril's instruction reflects the popular methods of the day. He is in part apologetic, part doctrinal. But there is a clear structure to his catechesis based on the tenets of the Creed. To the people of Jerusalem Cyril offered a pre-Lenten 'Procatechesis', followed by eighteen 'Catecheses' delivered during Lent. In these, Cyril spoke about such topics as God the Father, the all-powerful Creator of heaven and earth. To the newly-baptised (now known as 'neophytes', from the Greek: *neos*, new, and *phutos*, grown; *neophutos*, newly planted, seedling) Cyril delivered five 'Mystagogic Catecheses' in Easter week on the sacraments of initiation and the obligations of the Christian life.

The work of Cyril of Jerusalem offers a clear picture of catechesis in the fourth century. The Creed had become the standard reference point, and more and more emphasis was placed on commentaries on the Creed – knowledge of doctrine was assumed.

The lengthy period of preparation leading up to the celebration of the Easter Vigil and beyond, as described in detail in St Augustine's *De Catechizandis Rudibus*, gradually disappeared as significant changes took place within Christian communities. The rigorous testing and proving of candidates seemed to lose importance when Christianity became the official religion of the Roman Empire in 380 AD. It became fashionable to be a Christian, a social matter rather than a religious one. Christians were favoured and protected by the Roman emperors, and some people undoubtedly became Christians for motives that had little to do with faith. Although this initially led to an increase in the number of baptisms, this trend gradually changed. The reasons were varied: for some, the fact that catechumens were acknowledged to be Christians suggested there was no immediate need to be baptised. There was also concern over the severe penances that were now given in the sacrament of penance, and the idea that full forgiveness could only be received once after baptism. Hence many people delayed baptism until as near death as possible, including even Emperor Constantine himself.

From about the fifth century there was a gradual decline in the catechumenate. In many places it had been replaced by the widespread practice of infant baptism, and so where the catechumenate continued to exist it was often reduced to providing help for parents and godparents. The catechumenate as a period of moral and doctrinal preparation preceding the Easter baptismal celebration disappeared.

> The need for faith in the one to be baptised was supplied by the sponsor, who spoke on the infant's behalf. The role of the sponsor thus underwent a change: rather than being a guarantor of the candidate's faith and way of life, the sponsor now became a guardian of the child's faith after baptism, responsible for the Christian upbringing of the child.[2]

Over the course of a few centuries the whole process of initiation had subtly changed. Almost unnoticed, instruction had shifted from something pre-baptismal to being post-baptismal and was aimed largely at those who had already been baptised.

Handing on faith – the basics

From the historical snapshot seen up to now, and with other developments in the Church between the fifth and ninth centuries, it is possible to indicate the essential elements of early catechetical instruction. As the Church expanded throughout Europe, there was increasing emphasis on basic preaching to convert the pagans. For people like St Patrick, St Augustine of Canterbury and St Boniface, this would have meant convincing people that idol worship was useless, that there was a need to believe in God as Creator, in his Son who died to save us, and to put into action the message of the gospel. All this was signified by baptism, although it was not often seen as initiation into a community.

Candidates who wished to be baptised needed to memorise the Creed and the 'Pater noster' (the Our Father). These two texts were explained to them during Lent. Many local church councils from the eighth century onwards required the clergy to preach regularly on the Lord's Prayer and the Creed – a sign that these were *the* two basic catechetical texts, and that the homily was still the basic form of religious instruction.[3] The Council of Beziers in the thirteenth century declared:

> parish priests see to it that they explain to the people on Sundays the articles of faith in simple and clear fashion so that no one may claim a veil of ignorance ... Children too from seven upwards, brought to Church by their parents on Sundays and feasts, shall be instructed in the Catholic faith, and parents shall teach them *Mary's Salutation, Our Father* and *Creed*.[4]

From the time of the eighth and ninth centuries more written manuals on the faith were produced. The 'question-and-answer' format that Augustine did not approve of as a teaching device was now becoming very popular as the basic tool for catechetical instruction. The introduction of this method is sometimes attributed to Alcuin of York (*c.* 740–804), who wrote nearly three hundred questions in his biblical treatise, *Interrogationes et responsiones in Genesin*. Texts of this nature seemed to be taking catechesis in a direction which focused on assimilating vast quantities of information, simply teaching about religion from a textbook.

Many of these 'question-and-answer' textbooks were addressed to the clergy – to those who would be teaching the faith – to aid them in their teaching. One such famous text was the twelfth-century *Elucidarium*, attributed to Honorius, a popular theologian of the time. The *Elucidarium* is one of the earliest surveys of Christian doctrine in the form of a dialogue between pupil and master. As one American author, Gerard Sloyan, stated, 'The *Elucidarium* has a distressingly modern ring to it in dozens of places. Surely it marks the death and burial of the patristic tradition in catechetics, just as it brings to the fore the theological answer-machine which, while claiming to deal in mysteries, does not seem to be aware of any'.[5]

It is important to understand what this means for catechetics. It represents a major shift in terms of the target audience, with resources now being produced exclusively for adults. The *Elucidarium* is not a child's book, yet it must have informed thousands of adults who, in turn, formed many children theologically. And the format for handing on faith is the simple 'question-and-answer' format:

> Disciple: 'What was the cause of the world's creation?'
> Master: 'The goodness of God, so that there might be those on whom to confer His grace.'
> Disciple: 'How was it done?'
> Master: ' "He spoke and all things were made" (Ps. 22:9).'
> Disciple: 'And did He use words?'
> Master: 'For God, to speak is to create all things by His Word, that is, in the Son; which is why we read, "In wisdom have you done all things" (Ps. 103:24).'[6]

Scripture, as we can see from the above, is used as a proof-text to support a particular position. There is no attempt to reflect on Scripture in any way.

The *Elucidarium* had firmly introduced the 'question-and-answer' format and thereby encouraged people to memorise short, succinct texts. The direction of catechesis, of teaching the faith, had been firmly set. Again, Gerard Sloyan notes:

> And yet the net effect of the *Elucidarium* is slightly depressing, for religious encyclopedism is well in the saddle and a cloud no bigger than a man's hand is on the horizon. It will burst when 483 distinct questions and answers have been assembled in one book. (In one national catechism the number is seven hundred.) The technique is deadly because it lends itself to memorization so readily.[7]

St Thomas Aquinas and catechesis

No look at catechetical development would be complete without a glance at the notable contribution of St Thomas Aquinas (*c.* 1225–74). While he may not immediately seem to be an obvious candidate for furthering catechesis in the Middle Ages, there is a clear and valuable structure to his work that was to provide a foundation for many catechetical homilies.

In Lent 1273 St Thomas preached nearly sixty sermons in the church of St Dominic in Naples. He provided a methodical series of reflections on the Apostles' Creed, the Lord's Prayer and the Ten Commandments. Aware of his congregation, it would seem that Thomas' sermons were never longer than half an hour. He used experience to illustrate his talks and spoke of the 'three things necessary to man for salvation; namely, knowledge of what to believe (*scientia credendorum*), what to wish for (*desiderandorum*), and what to do (*operandorum*). The first is taught in the Creed . . . the second in the Lord's Prayer; the third in the Law . . .'. For Thomas, catechesis stems from the message, and his threefold structure was to be the definitive source for many sermons for years to come.

REFLECTION

- Typology, seeing Old Testament figures as foreshadowing the Christian era, became a very popular catechetical tool. Can you think how it might be useful today? Does it make the Bible more accessible?
- By the end of the fourth century it was 'fashionable' to be a Christian. What comment would you make about such an approach which may have had little to do with faith? What might be said to any people today whose motives for turning to religion might have little to do with faith? Can you think of situations where this is true?
- In what ways do you think the sermon or homily hands on faith? Is it a vehicle for teaching?
- How can a question-and-answer format hand on faith? What are the advantages and disadvantages?

2 *From Catechesis to Catechisms*

Handing on faith to those who had never heard the Christian message, the *rudes* as Augustine had called them, was a complex task. Preaching remained an important vehicle for this, but other elements of church life also complemented this endeavour. Religious art became a wonderful visual catechetical tool, with cathedrals and churches full of pictures, statues and stained glass depicting stories from the Bible and the lives of the saints. The majority of people could 'read' these images: pictures, stained glass windows, wayside crosses and altar-pieces.

These images literally 'came to life' with the flourishing of religious drama, which became a great vehicle for catechesis. In England and France in the Middle Ages there was the development of what became known as 'Mystery' or 'Miracle' plays, dramatising first of all the events of Holy Week and Easter and then other events from the Bible. Legendary subjects were also dramatised, such as the life of the Virgin Mary and the Harrowing of Hell, when Christ descended into hell after his death to defeat the powers of evil. In North England, most famously at York, there was also a series of Corpus Christi plays given processionally on wagons used as movable stages.

Some experts have called this visual dimension 'catechesis by immersion', since it formed the imagination and encouraged not so much an intellectual approach to faith but a pious way of life which touched people's emotions:

> ... explanations of faith concepts were given not merely by showing images, but also through dramatisation, by making people weep or laugh. People were moved in faith when their emotions were aroused. Popular missions used

this learning process as early as the fifteenth century. Vigorous and racy language was used in combination with the image. The combination goaded people to think and to feel.[1]

But dependence on oral communication of the faith, the centuries-old wisdom handed down in different ways by different personalities, was about to be shattered. The Church's very culture and way of working was to be transformed for ever. Sometime between 1440 and 1456 Johann Gutenberg introduced printing to Europe and in 1457 the first dated book, a psalter, was produced. Handing on faith was never to be the same.

Printed manuals: catechisms

It is said today, with some reason, that if you were to ask a number of people to preach on the same topic or biblical text, you would not get two sermons the same. A similar situation existed throughout the fifteenth century, with handing on faith in the sermon very much dependent on the vagaries and interpretation of the preacher. Personalities and circumstances were extremely influential. There was also a growing ignorance among the clergy, as shown by this remarkable snapshot of parish life in England:

> As late as 1551 the new Bishop of Gloucester, John Hooper (d. 1555), was dismayed when visitation records for his parish clergy indicated that out of 311 clergy: 168 were unable to repeat the Decalogue, 9 could not count the Commandments, and 33 were unable to locate them in Scripture; 10 clergy could not repeat the Lord's Prayer, 9 could not locate it in the Bible, and 34 were unable to name its author.[2]

It was partly to combat this ignorance and lack of uniformity in preaching and teaching that a number of theologians in Europe began to publish manuals addressed to specific groups, particularly children.

One of the great advocates of this type of catechesis was the chief protagonist of the Reformation Martin Luther (1483–1546). Although Luther is more renowned for the views which set in motion the Protestant Reformation, he is also remembered as an important scholar with distinctive views on handing on faith. Some of his earliest catechetical writings, dating from the time when Luther was still a Catholic, were made into charts for use in home, school and parish, and in 1520 he published a *Brief Form of the Ten Commandments, the Creed and the Lord's Prayer*. Martin Luther was excommunicated in 1521 and eight years later he produced his *Kleiner Katechismus* (Small Catechism) for laity and children, and the *Grosser Katechismus* (Greater Catechism) for clergy. These became the foundation for religious instruction in the home and parish and were so popular that within forty years one hundred thousand copies of the *Kleiner Katechismus* had been printed.

In his preface to this work, Luther outlined the process of handing on faith, making it clear that the catechist's role was that of teacher, explaining what had been learned and memorised:

> It is necessary to make the pupils and the people learn by heart the formulas chosen to be included in the little catechism, without changing a single syllable. As for those who refuse to learn word by word, tell them that they are denying Christ and are not Christians. Do not accept them at the Lord's Supper. Do not let them present a child for baptism. Send them to the Pope, to the Official Principal and to the devil himself . . . When the children know these texts well, they must also be taught their meaning, so that they will understand what the words mean. Take all the time you need, because it is not a question of explaining all the points at the same time, but of taking them one after another. Take the great catechism therefore and give a more fully developed and extended explanation.[3]

One of Luther's aims here, which is still a challenge of great importance today, was to make the family the centre of learning. Parents were responsible for their children's catechesis, nurturing Christian faith in the home. Luther was indicating to parents that handing on faith was not just a matter of good example but also required systematic teaching which could be provided by a thorough use of his *Kleiner Katechismus*. The method, which was to become the definitive mode for learning the faith for centuries to come, was simple: sentences from the *Katechismus* were to be repeated and memorised.

The subject matter, too, was straightforward. Luther's work followed the simple structure that had been in use for hundreds of years, beginning with the Ten Commandments ('so that he feels and sees what he can do and what he cannot do . . . and thus knows himself to be a sinner and a wicked man'), and going on to the Creed ('which shows him and teaches him where he may find the remedy') and the Lord's Prayer ('which teaches him how to ask for this grace'). To this Luther added something about the sacraments of baptism, confession and Eucharist, and various prayers. Throughout, he used Scripture wherever possible. Indeed, he felt that the Bible was so important that he had translated it into German, publishing the New Testament in 1522. Like the *Katechismus*, the German Bible became a fundamental text for religious instruction in the home, making catechesis and catechisms biblically based.

Luther's influence in catechesis cannot be underestimated. By the end of the sixteenth century his *Kleiner Katechismus* had been translated into seventeen European languages. More importantly, the whole nature of religious instruction had changed. Parents had a key role and were themselves taught by priests still using the sermon as the chief means of teaching. With catechisms widely available throughout Europe there was a uniformity of both doctrine and knowledge, since everyone simply repeated the same formulae memorised through the question-and-answer format which had now become the norm. For the first time there was some form of systematic religious education and what mattered was knowing the catechism by heart. 'Thus, it was possible to write at the beginning of the sixteenth century that "another kind of Christian is in the process of being born". That new Christian was a Christian of uniform knowledge and practices, a replica of Christian teachers. He or she had been subjected to formulas and was not a creative and mystical Christian . . .'[4]

More Catechisms and the Catholic response

Luther had initiated what is now termed a 'period of catechisms'. In 1555/6 a Dutch Jesuit, Peter Canisius (1521–97),
published three catechisms for different age groups: the *Maior*
for students, the *Minus* for children, and the *Minor* for ado-
lescents. Ten years before the publication of this 'graded
catechism', the Catholic bishops had already begun to meet at
Trent, in northern Italy, in response to the effects of the Protestant Reformation sweeping through Germany and other parts
of Europe. The bishops saw an urgent need to produce their
own catechism to counter what they perceived to be the her-
etical ideas contained in the popular catechisms now being
published by many of the reformers.

At the early sessions of the Council of Trent in 1546, discussion centred on the possibility of publishing something
similar to Luther's *Kleiner Katechismus*, a catechism for children
and 'uninstructed adults'. This idea was abandoned in favour
of something that could be used by priests 'to nourish and
strengthen the faithful with sound and wholesome doctrine, as
with the food of life. For false prophets have gone forth into
the world, to corrupt the minds of the faithful with various and
strange doctrines'.[5] The Council Fathers at the Council of Trent
were 'anxious to apply some healing remedy to so great and
pernicious an evil', and in 1566 Pope Pius V published the
Catechismus ex Decretis Concilii Tridentini ad Parachos, commonly
known as the *Roman Catechism*. Although the chief task of the
Council had been to clarify and restate Catholic doctrine, it had
also been deemed necessary 'to issue, for the instruction of the
faithful in the very rudiments of the faith, a form and method
to be followed in all churches by those to whom are lawfully
entrusted the duties of pastor and teacher'.[6]

Here was a catechism for the instruction of the instructors,
ensuring uniformity in 'form and method': 'that, as there is *one
Lord, one faith*, there may also be one standard and prescribed
form of propounding the dogmas of faith, and instructing
Christians in all the duties of piety'.[7] Although the *Roman Catechism* was not question-and-answer in style it still retained the
basic structure of Apostles' Creed, the Sacraments, the Ten

Commandments, and the Lord's Prayer. The methodology advocated by the *Roman Catechism* is interesting. For a 'text-book' so rigid in doctrine and discipline one might think that the method encouraged would be equally strict. On the contrary, priests are reminded that

> age, capacity, manners and condition must be borne in mind . . . The priest must not imagine that those committed to his care are all on the same level, so that he can follow one fixed and unvarying method of instruction to lead all in the same way to knowledge and true piety . . . Hence the necessity of considering who they are that have occasion for milk, who for more solid food, and of affording to each such nourishment of doctrine as may give *spiritual increase* . . .[8]

From an educational standpoint, the *Roman Catechism* might be considered way ahead of its time. It moved away from question-and-answer and the memorization of texts that such a method implied and, indeed, encouraged; it promoted a learning process which acknowledged people's different starting-points; since the homily was still the major vehicle for instruction, the *Roman Catechism* recognised priests as crucial to the whole process of learning and was addressed directly to them. It stated that priests must preach on Sundays and thereby instruct the faithful. In asking priests to teach in this way the *Roman Catechism* recognised, too, that learning was a life-long process. Furthermore, the Council ordered the establishment of a seminary in every diocese for the proper training of clergy.

However, in ensuring that the doctrines of the Catholic Church were taught properly, the *Roman Catechism* lost sight of one of Luther's great achievements, that of placing catechesis in the heart of the family. The instructors were clearly priests, not parents, and it seems the *Roman Catechism* was concerned solely with them. In fact, there is evidence to suggest that the role of the head of the family was to attend church to hear the sermon and then retell it to the household after dinner.[9] Handing on faith had become very different.

REFLECTION

* 'One catechism, one translation of the Bible, the Vulgate, and one truth, that of Trent. The human mind is called to go to sleep. Everything that moves is shot at'.[10] What does this say about faith? Does this suggest that faith is merely an intellectual concept or is it really something dynamic? Is this fair on Trent and the *Roman Catechism*?

* Looking back on the *Roman Catechism*, one English expert in the field of catechetics said that it did not succeed in what it set out to do by reaching every adult Catholic: 'The theology was spread too thick, the book was too unwieldy, the sentences too lengthy, the whole effort of adaptation too much for the ordinary priest'.[11] Does this sound any warnings about textbook catechetics and the challenge of adaptation?

Yet more Catechisms

The commission which was finally responsible for the *Roman Catechism* had been led by the Cardinal Archbishop of Milan, Charles Borromeo (1538–84). When he was appointed to Milan in 1560 he set about implementing many of the decrees of the Council of Trent. However, one of his most important tasks was the reorganisation of the 'Company of Christian Doctrine' which had been established in Milan in 1536 to provide religious education for children, young people and uneducated adults at a time when schools were largely for the rich and the level of religious education was at an all-time low. The 'Confraternity of Christian Doctrine', as it became known, had a large number of schools in the Milan archdiocese run by lay people. Charles Borromeo wrote a lengthy *Constitution and Rules of the Confraternity and School of Christian Doctrine for Use in the Province of Milan*. It was a text ahead of its time, repeating the need to adapt religious instruction to different ages that had been outlined in the *Roman Catechism*. The *Constitution* also listed some principles that seem obvious to those reading about them at a distance of four hundred years, but revolutionary for the time: that groups should not exceed ten participants, that sessions should only last forty-five minutes and be followed by a discussion, and prayers together should end the session. The Archbishop of Milan also insisted that teachers be examined before being allowed to take any lessons, thus ensuring that they were properly qualified to instruct people in the faith. The Confraternity was such a success that when St Charles Borromeo died in 1584 there were more than 3,000 lay teachers providing instruction for more than 40,000 children and adults in the schools.[12]

Catechisms were still widely used throughout Europe and were in fact becoming more popular. Just before the end of the sixteenth century, the Italian Jesuit Robert Bellarmine (1542–1621) published a *Dottrina Cristiana Breve da Impararsi a Mente* (Summary of Christian Doctrine to be Memorised) in the form of teachers' questions and pupils' responses. Aimed at children and the uneducated, this work proved very popular and was translated into other languages. Bellarmine's work shows that instruction was now firmly set in the mould of question-and-answer and memorising the responses.

Looking to England, the same pattern in handing on faith was beginning to emerge. Following the example of Peter Canisius, a Dr Laurence Vaux of Manchester published a *Christian Doctrine Necessarie for Children and Ignorante People* (1567), while the most famous catechism in England was that published in 1759 by Bishop Richard Challoner, entitled *Abridgement of Christian Doctrine*.

Richard Challoner (1691–1781) trained for the priesthood at Douai College in France and went directly from student to professor to vice-president. He was consecrated bishop in 1741 and was a prodigious author. In his *Abridgement of Christian Doctrine*, Challoner reflected the work of his English predecessors in this field, especially Dr Vaux. Catechisms were now the standard means of religious education in the English-speaking world. In England and Ireland, where Catholic schools were forbidden under the penal laws, catechisms were ideal. These small handbooks could be easily hidden and the question-and-answer format made the text easy to memorise. For more than a hundred years, Challoner's catechism was the basic tool for instruction and it provided the basis for the 1898 *A*

Catechism of Christian Doctrine, popularly known as the 'Penny Catechism'.

The 'Penny Catechism' was the foundation of much of the religious instruction that took place, eventually, in schools, parishes and homes, and it is still used by some today. Its opening questions and answers – 'Who made you? God made me. Why did God make you? God made me to know him, love him and serve him in this world, and to be happy with him for ever in the next' – were quoted at the start of this book and may have been familiar to many people. However, some might argue that handing on faith had been reduced to the idea of producing cheap textbooks that children could learn off by heart, since all they needed to know about faith was contained in the prayers and 370 questions and answers of *A Catechism of Christian Doctrine*.

Knowledge of doctrine had become primary and this influence could be seen in America, where, in 1885, a book was published which has been referred to as 'possibly the most important single influence on the doctrinal understanding of many generations of U.S. Roman Catholics'.[13] The book *A Catechism of Christian Doctrine, Prepared and Enjoined by Order of the Third Plenary Council of Baltimore* – which became shortened to the *Baltimore Catechism* – was a question-and-answer text aimed at children and young people. Earlier attempts to publish catechisms in the United States included an attempt to adapt Challoner's catechism, *A Short Abridgment of Christian Doctrine. Newly Revised for the Use of the Catholic Church in the United States of America*. This was authorised by Archbishop John Carroll of Baltimore (1735–1815). By the time of the early nineteenth century the American bishops were motivated by a strong desire for uniformity of expression and orthodoxy. Many dioceses had produced their own catechisms and translations of a number of German catechisms were also being used. In 1850, the Bishop of Cincinnati decreed that the German catechisms in use should not be reprinted, and nearly twenty years later the Second Plenary Council of Baltimore called for a standard catechism in all dioceses. The same appeal was made again at the Third Plenary Council of Baltimore (November 1884) and this time the request bore fruit. The *Baltimore Catechism* was approved by the Cardinal Archbishop of Baltimore in April 1885. It became the official text for religious instruction of Catholic children in the United States of America.

The *Baltimore Catechism* was exclusively question-and-answer and gave rise to a whole series of graded books for the different age groups using the text. This was an important development. Within a year of the publication of the *Baltimore Catechism* an abridged version had appeared, to be followed by illustrated editions and a series of manuals with more or fewer questions depending on the target audience. In subsequent years, religious education resources in the United States were rooted in the *Baltimore Catechism* – a text which, after further changes were made, was approved by the Vatican in 1941.

By the middle of the nineteenth century printed texts were at the heart of catechesis. But, just as the invention of printing had had a dramatic effect on the direction of catechesis in the fifteenth century, so another factor was to have equally significant consequences in the nineteenth century. While Martin Luther had emphasised the role of the family in catechesis and St Charles Borromeo had encouraged the laity to instruct people through the Confraternity of Christian Doctrine, compulsory schooling was to reduce catechesis/instruction to a classroom activity. Religious education was henceforth to be identified with school. Although this did mean that all pupils could receive regular religious education, it was clear that a distinction had been made – albeit unwittingly – between faith as something intellectual and faith as something to be lived out each day, with consequences beyond the school curriculum and timetable. A doctrinal, even academic emphasis had won the day:

> When schools took over more and more from parents the task of teaching religion . . . religion as a life to be lived gradually succumbed to the notion of religion as a series of propositions to be committed to memory after careful analysis . . . It is quite possible for the child catechized 'in the faith' to withhold his personal consent or simply to go through a process of learning about something which has no effect on his personal faith.[14]

Catechism and Council

Towards the end of the nineteenth century, the First Vatican Council was convoked by Pope Pius IX to deal with a variety of subjects, including faith and dogma, church discipline and law, religious orders, and relations between Church and State. The Council met from December 1869 to October 1870 and in February 1870 the bishops were presented with a schema entitled 'The Compilation and Adoption of a Single Short Catechism for the Universal Church'. The aim was clear: to replace the many catechisms in use with a single text obligatory for the whole Church.

The debate that ensued revealed the importance the bishops attached to religious education. Some saw the schema as an attempt at Roman centralization and were upset at the idea that such a catechism might be obligatory. It went against the right of bishops to edit their own catechisms and raised the whole question of the relationship between bishops and the Holy See, which had subtly become the real focal point for the debate. As one Hungarian archbishop put it: 'To catechize the people is one of the great duties and rights of a bishop; if a catechism is dictated to us, our sermons will be dictated next'.[15]

Debate among the bishops highlighted the whole question of unity and uniformity. Some bishops supported the idea of one text, while others felt that a single text would not be able to respond to particular pastoral problems unique to each part of the Church. They posed the question which is still raised today: how can a single text produced by a central authority respond to the needs of a multicultural society? Ultimately, support at the First Vatican Council was for centralization, and the proposal was for a single catechism intended for children and to be learnt by heart. However, the proposal never reached a final vote due to the outbreak of the Franco-Prussian War, and the Council was suspended in October 1870. A 'universal catechism' became unfinished business.

The debate at the First Vatican Council had raised many issues. What became clear was that an increased centralization would mean that the role of bishops in religious education was to change. Bureaucracy took over, and accountability was to the directives of Rome. Uniformity had become canonical rather than catechetical.

Ideas about instruction, catechesis and handing on faith were to undergo a gradual revolution in the twentieth century, a revolution reflected in the documents that were produced. But, at the turn of the century, the picture was clear. Catechisms were *the* means of instruction, with question-and-answer and memorization the preferred teaching method used exclusively in schools. Family catechesis had all but disappeared. Preaching at a catechetical congress in Chicago in 1951, the former Apostolic Delegate to the United States, Archbishop (later Cardinal) Cicognani gave the catechism unqualified praise and summed up the whole approach to instruction and handing on faith: 'No human book can compare with the catechism in certitude or in power. It transforms tender children into sure theologians . . . The catechism is a fortress against atheism and a bulwark for the freedom and the life of man'.[16]

REFLECTION

- What differences can you imagine between catechesis in the family and catechesis in the classroom? How would faith be handed on in these environments?
- My father's preparation for Confirmation consisted mainly in memorising the answers to questions 262–5 of *A Catechism of Christian Doctrine*. What image of faith does that give?
- Can faith be taught from a textbook?
- 'Religious Instruction' – 'Religious Education': what's in a name?
- In what ways do you think a centrally produced text can respond to worldwide needs?
- How would you think of the differences between uniformity and unity? What are the advantages and disadvantages of each?

The changes begin

The first rumblings of discontent about instruction in faith by learning texts came from the application of secular educational theories to catechetics. Before the First World War, German-speaking countries led the way in searching for a more effective method of learning and they turned to the educational insights of Johann Friedrich Herbart (1776–1841). He had proposed a theory of teaching based on how children learn:

> Firstly, they perceive through their senses and imagination. Secondly, they understand through their mind or intellect. Thirdly, they act out or put into practice what they have understood, thereby bringing into play their emotions and their will. If this is how children learn then, Herbart suggests, teaching should consist of three corresponding steps, called Presentation, Explanation and Application.[17]

When applied to religious education, this method would envisage a religious lesson beginning with the presentation of a story, possibly from the Bible, followed by an explanation of the doctrinal truth in the story, and concluding with its application to daily life. This theory was approved at a Catechetical Congress in Munich in 1928 and became known as the 'Munich Method'.

Although it never gained universal acceptance, the Munich Method had at least begun to introduce significant changes into the world of catechetics and Christian education in general. It was a sign that there was a reaction against the catechism as the definitive form of teaching religion and that there was a shift from memorising to understanding. The Munich Method also attempted to make learning a more active process, and introduced learning theory into catechesis.

This development was a reaction against the method of learning implied by the question-and-answer format of the catechism. The next significant change came about because of a focus on the content of the catechism, challenging the text not only as a deficient educational method but also as an inadequate summary of Christian faith. Catechetics was in some way divorced from 'real life':

Most people know all the sacraments; they know about the Person of Christ as well as about Our Lady, Peter and Paul, Adam and Eve, and a good many others. They know enough about the commandments of God and of the Church. But what is lacking among the faithful is a sense of unity, seeing it all as a whole, an understanding of the wonderful message of divine grace. All they retain of Christian doctrine is a string of dogmas and moral precepts, threats and promises, customs and rites, tasks and duties imposed on unfortunate Catholics, whilst the non-Catholic gets off free of them.[18]

The great proponent of this shift in emphasis from method to content was an Austrian Jesuit, Josef Andreas Jungmann (1889–1975). His foundational book, *The Good News and Our Presentation of the Faith*, was originally published in 1936 (an abridged version in English, *The Good News Yesterday and Today*, did not appear until 1962, because the original was withdrawn from circulation after pressure from the Holy Office in Rome) and encouraged a return to the basic message of Christ, the *kerygma* (a Greek term meaning 'preaching'). Jungmann argued that the language of the catechism was dry and uninspiring, the doctrinal formulations of scholastic theology. Christianity was not simply a system of truths or set of rules that needed to be memorised, but a living message of Good News. He presented faith as something dynamic and active, not arid doctrine.

Jungmann also brought back the concept of 'salvation history', looking at God's plan for humanity expressed through his self-revelation in history and until the end of time.

Catechetics, then, cannot be seen as the retailing of a doctrine by *teachers*, themselves more or less involved in it all, but rather the utterance of witnesses who communicate and pass on the message which is their very breath of life. At the center of this message is a *person* – Jesus Christ, the salvation of mankind. So catechetics must be *personalized*, following the behavior of human intercourse, and *christocentric*, that is, molding all its elements around the central figure of Christ.[19]

At the heart of the Kerygmatic Movement, as it is known, was the idea that catechetics was to be rooted not in doctrinal formulae but in the life, death and resurrection of Jesus Christ. Seen in this way, the Scriptures became not stories to illustrate doctrine, but a revelation of the person of Christ. His message was presented in the Scriptures, in liturgical celebration, in Church teaching, and in the witness of the life of the Christian community.

Jungmann was greatly influenced by developments taking place at the time in biblical and liturgical studies. With his own developments in the field of catechetics through the Kerygmatic Movement, a whole new spirit was breathed into the unity of Church life in many parts of Europe. Liturgy, the Bible and catechesis were not seen as separate parts of a whole, but as a unity of faith. Catechetical renewal was renewing Church life. 'Catechetics shatters the childish bounds of little catechisms and springs to the forefront in the life of the Church. As the Vatican Council II will tell us, catechetics is the first of all the means used by the Church to fulfill its teaching role'.[20]

Jungmann's work made the very word 'catechesis' fashionable again, rooting it in the Church's pastoral mission. People began to speak of 'catechesis' rather than 'religious education'. This latter took place almost exclusively in school, whereas catechesis extended into the parish and the home. To borrow a phrase that is perhaps overused today, the vision of Jungmann was that catechesis was seen as education *to* and *in* the faith, not just instruction *about* the faith.

Canon Drinkwater and The Sower

Changes in catechetical method sweeping across Europe were also beginning to make their presence felt in England. Religious instruction in the early part of the twentieth century was still dominated by the 'Penny Catechism', the question-and-answer text based on Bishop Challoner's 1759 *An Abridgement of Christian Doctrine*. Needless to say, learning was by heart.

Catechetical reform in England is often attributed to the work of one man, Francis H. Drinkwater (1886–1982). He was ordained priest for the Archdiocese of Birmingham in 1910 and made some interesting comments about his first attempts in preparing seven-year-olds for their first confession and first communion so that these sacraments could be

> ... a spiritual and psychology reality. In this task, and with those children, the catechism was evidently not going to be any help, so we left it aside and learned how to teach them what was necessary in their own simple language. I always look back to this decree of Pius X [*Quam singulari*, admitting seven-year-olds to Holy Communion] as the real beginning of catechetical reform, for it forced us all back on the psychological realities of childhood.[21]

Canon Drinkwater was clearly aiming to link instruction with the age and intellectual and spiritual capacity of the child. In 1921 he established a monthly review, *The Sower*, and through this managed to express many of his ideas. He became a great advocate of the Munich Method in catechesis. While he accepted the catechism as a traditional summary of Christian doctrines, Canon Drinkwater recognised such knowledge to be only one feature of understanding and living Christian faith. This point was made very clear to him during his time as an army chaplain in the First World War, where he discovered that although many of the soldiers had forgotten the abstract formulae of faith they had been taught they still retained some of the practical aspects of living their faith. Canon Drinkwater spoke of the importance of using language that children can understand and was convinced that the system of 'parrot learning', as he called it, was simply imparting knowledge that the mind was not yet ready to receive.

> From the beginning it was seen that religious instruction is a good deal more than the imparting of a certain amount of doctrine. First, the child is a living, growing creature and demands activity. Hence the emphasis on life, not only in the sense that the child takes in knowledge through living but in the sense that the whole purpose of instruction is to form him for life after he has left school.[22]

The revolutionary ideas proposed by Canon Drinkwater were

introduced into the archdiocese with some degree of protest. In 1929, the Sower Scheme, as it was now known, became the official religious instruction scheme throughout Birmingham's Catholic schools. The catechism was to be learned only by senior children, thus leaving the junior school open to new methods of handing on faith.

Continuing change

Catechesis had undergone remarkable changes due to clear reflection on the content and method employed. Further change was to come about due to what was called the 'Anthropological/Experiential Approach'. Attention was now focused on the recipients of catechesis, those to whom the Word of God was addressed. The starting-point was to become the person's own life and circumstances rather than a document of faith. An inductive methodology meant that life and human experience were seen as openings to faith. The anthropological approach aimed to enlighten experience through faith, with an emphasis on content being appropriate for the various stages in human growth and faith development. A number of key words and phrases sum up the experiential approach to faith. There is talk of 'relevance', of 'stages' of faith, of using 'a language with which people are familiar', and of things being 'pupil-centred' (although the school was now no longer seen as the only place for religious education/catechesis).

The influences for this approach to catechetics were to be found in studies in developmental psychology, depth psychology, and faith and moral development. The research and insights of psychologists such as Piaget, Kohlberg and Fowler were applied to religious instruction and resulted in a more life-centred, experiential approach to the teaching of religion. Such an approach was very popular in France, where Fr Joseph Colomb (1902–79) produced a three-volume *Catechisme progressif*, in which everything was arranged according to the age and capacity of the child, not according to a logical, systematic theology. He was concerned about what he termed the 'double fidelity' of being faithful to God but also to humanity. The implication was that catechesis must respect and take into account human maturity.

Another French author, the Dominican Pierre-André Liégé, wrote about the importance of considering the environment in which catechesis takes place. He saw France as a country marked by a lack of belief, a de-christianized nation. In this context Liege introduced the word 'pre-evangelization' to signify the groundwork that needed to be done before people would be receptive to the kerygmatic proclamation of the Good News.

A time of catechetical conferences

The many debates about catechesis and religious education were brought into a sharp focus by the Austrian Father Johannes Hofinger, who helped to organise a series of six International Catechetical Study Weeks between 1959 and 1968. These were held at Nijmegen in Holland (1959), Eichstätt in West Germany (1960), Bangkok in Thailand (1962), Katigondo in Uganda (1964), Manila in the Philippines (1967), and Medellin in Colombia (1968).

Although it is beyond the scope of this work to go into detail about what each Study Week achieved, it is worth noting some important developments. The 1960 meeting at Eichstätt had the theme 'Catechetics and the Missions', thus firmly rooting catechesis in the mission of the Church. There was great support for the Kerygmatic Movement, although missionaries began to reflect on the whole nature of *inculturation*. This idea echoed the 'double-fidelity' theme advocated by Joseph Colomb. Missionaries spoke of the need to understand the cultures in which they were working and to proclaim the gospel message in ways that those cultures would understand.

Such an idea received enthusiastic support at the 1962 Study Week in Bangkok which set great store by the need for 'pre-evangelization'. It was clear the gospel message needed to be adapted to the environment in which it was proclaimed. The modern phrase reflecting this approach is to 'take people where they are at'. Two years later, the 'Pan-African Seminar' in

Uganda endorsed this anthropological approach to catechesis with its stress on pre-evangelization, adaptation and inculturation. More and more emphasis was placed on the formation of adult Christians.

The Asian Study Week in Manila (1967) was the first to be held after the conclusion of the Second Vatican Council, and in some ways reflected many of the concerns of the Council, in particular the relationship between Catholicism and the values expressed by other religions. Such an approach signified a new openness in the area of catechesis, implying the dialogue of a two-way process of being evangelised and evangelising.

This recognition of the changing situation in the world was at the heart of the Latin-American Study Week held at Medellin, Columbia, in 1968. What was new about Medellin was its outlook not just on the individual to be catechised but also the community and human development within that community. This was a call not just to 'know' the truth but a call to 'action', to live out the truth of faith. True catechesis was also a call to change society, to find a new way of expressing the gospel in society. Doubtless this stemmed from a reflection on the situation in Latin-America itself – Christian in name but marked by injustice and oppression. Hence, the first step of catechesis was to look at the situation not just of the individual but of society itself, so that the message of salvation would be rooted in a particular situation. Catechesis aimed at improving life now, not just promising an idealistic, spiritual future. Biblical catechesis meant making the message present now in society, bringing together the 'sacred' and the 'profane'. Revelation is about daily life. This is an extension of the anthropological approach to catechesis which had moved in the direction of acknowledging that to speak about God was to speak about humanity, that there could be no separation between faith and life. It was very much an examination of the social demands of the gospel.

Key words and phrases from the Medellin Study Week would be 'community', 'inculturation', the tension between the 'already' and the 'not yet' of the kingdom of God, and the idea of the gospel in action.

Medellin challenged catechesis to come to grips with the political and socio-economic order which shapes the religious attitudes of communities as well as individuals. Picking up a theme from Vatican II, it asserted that there can be no lasting renewal in catechesis unless there is reform in the Church and in society at large and that one of the tasks of catechesis is to work for that reform.[23]

REFLECTION

- The German theologian Paul Tillich (1886–1965) once said: 'Jesus does not call people to religion, but to life.' Is this just a clever phrase or an important point? Is there, should there be, a difference between religion and life?
- Looking back at the era of Congresses, what do you think they achieved?
- In the renewal of catechesis and the way it seems to be developing in this era, can you sense any problems? Can you think of anything that is being lost by development in this direction?
- Is the pace of development too quick?
- What does the anthropological approach add? How important is experience? Is it right to start with experience?

Catechesis and the Second Vatican Council

The First Vatican Council (1869–70) had proposed a single, universal catechism intended for children and to be learned by heart. The proposal was never fulfilled, although support for such a text remained. As the bishops gathered for the Second Vatican Council, nearly one hundred years after the First, there were still many requests for a single catechism. The Roman Curia, too, was keen for a document that would contain the basic teachings of the Catholic Church. This is an interesting fact, since at this time, as we have seen, the whole catechetical world was undergoing rapid developments concerning content and method in religious education. Indeed, it might be said that the notion of a single, universal catechism in the early 1960s is totally contrary to the signs offered by the anthropological approach to catechesis in full swing at that time. In the end, the Council did not continue with the proposals of the First Vatican Council for a universal catechism. Nor, however, did it issue a specific document on the subject of catechesis. Some bishops called instead for catechetical guidelines, a 'directory' that could be adapted locally and used in composing national directories.

Much of what the Second Vatican Council had to say about catechesis is reflected in its statements about the role of the bishop as a teacher of the faith, expressed in the *Decree on the Pastoral Office of Bishops in the Church*, promulgated in October 1965. This *Decree* stated clearly that one of the principal duties of the bishop was to proclaim the gospel of Christ: 'Bishops should present Christ's teaching in a manner relevant to the needs of the times, providing a response to those difficulties and problems which people find especially distressing and burdensome' (n. 13). The *Decree* went on:

> Bishops should also employ the various methods available nowadays for proclaiming christian doctrine. These are, first of all, preaching and catechetical instruction, which always hold pride of place ... Bishops should be especially concerned about catechetical instruction. Its function is to develop in women and men a living, explicit and active faith, enlightened by doctrine. It should be very carefully imparted, not only to children and adolescents but also to young people and even to adults. In imparting this instruction, the teachers must observe an order and method suited not only to the matter in hand but also to the character, the ability, the age and the lifestyle of their audience. This instruction should be based on holy scripture, tradition, liturgy, and on the teaching authority and life of the church. They should, furthermore, ensure that catechists are adequately prepared for their task, being well instructed in the doctrine of the church and possessing both a practical and theoretical knowledge of the laws of psychology and of educational method. They should take

steps to reestablish or to improve the adult catechumenate. (nn. 13–14)

The *Decree* ended by recommending that a 'directory for the catechetical instruction of the christian people' (n. 44) be drawn up, which would include the fundamental principles, organisation and resources for such instruction.

What the *Decree* was clearly acknowledging was the importance of inculturation. This was expressed directly in the *Decree on the Church's Missionary Activity*:

> The bishop should be, above all, a preacher of the faith who brings new disciples to Christ. To fulfil this noble task as he ought he must be fully acquainted with conditions among his flock and also with those notions about God which are current among his countrymen. He must take special account of those changes which have been brought about through urbanization, migration and religious indifferentism . . . Episcopal conferences should ensure that periodically there are refresher courses on the Bible and in spiritual and pastoral theology, so that amid all the change and flux the clergy will acquire a deeper knowledge of theology and of pastoral methods. (n. 20)

As we have seen, the journey of faith which had begun with the catechumenate in the early Church had changed dramatically down the centuries. Now, at the Second Vatican Council, the world's bishops called for a rediscovery of this journey of faith: 'The catechumenate for adults, divided into several distinct steps, is to be restored and brought into use at the discretion of the local Ordinary. By this means, the time of the catechumenate, which is destined for the requisite formation, may be sanctified by sacred rites to be celebrated at successive stages'.[24] But inculturation was not to be overlooked here, either: 'In mission countries, in addition to what is found in the christian tradition, those elements of initiation may be admitted which are already in use among every people . . .'[25]

One of the documents issued by the Council in 1965 was the *Declaration on Christian Education*. Although this important document proclaimed the basic principles of Christian education with particular reference to schools, it nevertheless said some important things about 'catechetical instruction', which 'illumines and strengthens the faith, develops a life in harmony with the spirit of Christ, stimulates a conscious and fervent participation in the liturgical mystery and encourages people to take an active part in the apostolate' (n. 4). The *Declaration* spoke of the 'inalienable right to education', which 'should be suitable to the particular destiny of the individuals, adapted to their ability, sex and national cultural traditions ... Due weight being given to the advances in psychological, pedagogical and intellectual sciences, children and young people should be helped to develop harmoniously their physical, moral and intellectual qualities' (n. 1).

The *Declaration on Christian Education* presented a holistic view of education which was reflected in many of the other Council documents. The *Constitution on the Sacred Liturgy* expressed the Church's wish that 'all the faithful should be led to take that full, conscious, and active part in liturgical celebrations which is demanded by the very nature of the liturgy' and therefore encouraged pastors to 'energetically set about achieving it through the requisite formation' (n. 14). The Council Fathers did note, however, that this first of all meant that the clergy needed proper liturgical training!

The need for proper formation was central to developing the vocation of lay Christians, as stated in the *Decree on the Apostolate of Lay People*:

> Education for the apostolate presupposes an integral human education suited to each one's abilities and conditions ... Besides spiritual formation, solid grounding in doctrine is required: in theology, ethics and philosophy, at least, proportioned to the age, condition and abilities of each one. The importance too of a general culture linked with a practical and technical training is something which should by no means be overlooked ... Training for the apostolate cannot consist only in being taught theory; on that account there is need, right from the start of training, to learn gradually and prudently to see all things in the light of faith, to judge and act always in its light, to improve

and perfect oneself by working with others, and in this way to enter actively into the service of the church. (n. 29)[26]

In its vision of education, the Second Vatican Council was reflecting the shifts we have seen in the world of catechetics in the years leading up to the Council. This could be seen above all in the *Pastoral Constitution on the Church in the Modern World*, published in December 1965. The desire for uniformity of previous years is replaced by the Church's responsibility of 'reading the signs of the times and interpreting them in the light of the Gospel . . . In language intelligible to every generation, it should be able to answer the ever recurring questions which people seek about the meaning of this present life and of the life to come . . .' (n. 4). Furthermore, 'theologians are now being asked, within the methods and limits of theological science, to develop more efficient ways of communicating doctrine to the people of today, for the deposit and the truths of faith are one thing, the manner of expressing them – provided their sense and meaning are retained – is quite another' (n. 62).

The world of handing on faith had moved from the days of memorization and dry, doctrinal formulae to a message rooted in the local cultures of the people of the day.

REFLECTION

- The Second Vatican Council saw the bishop as the chief catechist, the teacher of the faith in the local church. How is this worked out in practice? Can you think of times when you have seen this idea at work?
- The *Constitution on the Sacred Liturgy* called for the restoration of the catechumenate. Why do you think this was necessary? Do you think this was a good move? Has it made a diference locally? What has happened in your parish?
- The *Dogmatic Constitution on Divine Revelation* stated that the ministry of the Word, which includes catechetics, must be healthily nourished through the Word of Scripture (cf. n. 24). It says catechists and others 'should immerse themselves in the scriptures by constant spiritual reading and diligent study. For it must not happen that any of them become

"empty preachers of the word of God to others, not being
hearers of the word in their own hearts" ' (n. 25). Why is the
Bible so important in catechesis? Can you think of times
when explanations of the Scriptures have helped you or
puzzled you?

3 *The Decade of the* Directories

In the field of catechetics, the period from 1970–80 is often referred to as the 'Decade of the *Directories*', because, as a result of the Second Vatican Council, it saw the publication of many national catechetical directories, pastoral guidelines for handing on faith in a given culture. In acknowledging the importance of the bishop as the prime teacher of the faith in a diocese, the Council spoke of the bishop's task of overseeing the preparation of proper texts for the task of handing on faith:

> The preparation and publication of directories ... is integrally connected with the implementation of the thought and spirit of the Second Vatican Council in the local Church. The formal request for directories recognises the importance of the situation of the local Church in the task of handing on the faith. At the same time, it envisages a continuing dialogue between the local Church and the competent authority of a Roman Congregation (the Congregation for the Clergy) in the preparation of an official document such as a directory.[1]

What is a Directory?

As we have already noted, the First Vatican Council (1869–70) had proposed a universal catechism for children. Just under one hundred years later, as preparations for the Second Vatican Council began, there was still some enthusiasm for such a text. In drawing up the agenda for the Council, Pope John XXIII asked bishops and other church representatives to send in proposals for the agenda. It seems that only one bishop, the French Bishop Pierre-Marie Lacointe of Beauvais, asked for a directory

rather than a universal catechism. As the Second Vatican
Council progressed, his idea was welcomed.

Before the Council began, a number of schema were drafted
to set the agenda. Some of these schema treated various aspects
of catechesis and a final draft entitled *De cura animarum* ('The
Care of Souls') placed catechesis within the pastoral care of
bishops. This schema, or rather the ideas contained in it, eventually found its way into the *Decree on the Pastoral Office of
Bishops in the Church*, published in October 1965. In the final
paragraph of that document it is stated that

> The sacred synod further decrees that general directories
> concerning the care of souls be compiled for the use both of
> bishops and parish priests so that they may have definitive
> directives to guide them in the discharge of their particular
> pastoral function. A special directory should also be com-
> piled concerning the pastoral care of special groups of the
> faithful according to the various circumstances of different
> countries or regions, and also a directory for the catechet-
> ical instruction of the christian people in which the
> fundamental principles of this instruction and its organiz-
> ation will be dealt with and the preparation of books
> relating to it. (n. 44)

It could be said that the shift from uniformity to inculturation
had taken place, that what was acknowledged by the *Decree*
was the need to root the faith in the particular culture of the
local church. There was a move away from catechisms, even at
a diocesan level, towards establishing principles and guidelines
which would ensure the integrity of catechesis. Pope Paul VI
asked the Congregation of the Clergy to implement this work.

Even at a local level, such a shift was already beginning to
take place. In 1964, the French bishops had published a *Direct-
oire de la pastorale catéchétique*; and in 1966 the Dutch bishops
published *De Nieuwe Katechismus*, which became known as the
'Dutch Catechism'. The aim was to present 'anew to adults
the message which Jesus of Nazareth brought into the world,
to make it sound as new as it is ... in a form suitable to the
present day'. In the Foreword, the 'Dutch Catechism' stated

that it was a text faithful to the renewal of the Second Vatican Council:

> That is why it is called *A New Catechism*. But 'new' does not mean that some aspects of the faith have changed while all the rest remains as before. Had that been our object, we could simply have changed a few pages of the old catechism. But this is not the case. The whole message, the whole of the faith remains the same, but the approach, the light in which the faith is seen, is new. Everything that lives has both to remain itself and to renew itself. The message of Christ is a living thing, and hence this new type of catechism tries to present the faith of our fathers in a form suitable to the present day.[2]

This theme of renewal was taken up four years later by the Italian bishops, who published *Il rinnovamento della catechesi*, translated into English by the Australian Episcopal Conference under the title *The Renewal of the Education of Faith*.

While all these developments were taking place at a local level, the committees set up by Pope Paul VI were still working on a directory for catechesis. Bishops' Conferences throughout the world were consulted about the possible content of a catechetical directory and in May 1968 an international commission of experts began to draft a text. After numerous amendments and reworkings, the Sacred Congregation for the Doctrine of the Faith approved the text and the *General Catechetical Directory* was published on Easter Sunday, 11 April 1971.

The *GCD*, as it became popularly known, was revolutionary. It challenged the assumption that catechisms were the right way for handing on faith, the proper medium for catechesis. It reflected the developments of the international catechetical conferences held at Nijmegen, Eichstätt, Bangkok, Katigondo, Manila and Medellin. And it located catechesis very much within the ministry of the Word, biblically-based catechesis as opposed to a catechesis rooted in doctrines and rubrics.

The Introduction makes it very clear that this is a new departure, a completely new genre in catechesis: 'The purpose of this directory is to present the fundamental theological-pastoral principles, taken from the magisterium of the Church and especially the Second Vatican Council, for the guidance and better co-ordination of the ministry of the word. Hence the emphasis on theory, though the practical aspect is not neglected'. The aim, then, is to offer not a summary of Christian doctrine, but a 'proper understanding of the nature and purpose of catechesis . . . taking into account the recipients of catechesis and their social conditions'.

From the outset, the *Directory* mirrors much of what the Second Vatican Council had said about inculturation and the context for catechesis. It begins with a section entitled 'The Actual Problem', declaring:

> It must be borne in mind that if the Christian faith is to take root in successive cultures it must needs develop and must find new forms of expression . . . Today's believer is not in all respects like the believer of yesterday. Hence the need to ensure the continuity of the faith and at the same time proclaim the message of salvation in a new way. (n. 2)

Having examined some of the factors that affect the Church's proclamation of the gospel, the *Directory* goes on to link catechesis with revelation and evangelisation and states that the latter can precede or accompany catechesis. Indeed, the *Directory* adds the comment that 'every form of catechesis must involve evangelization' (n. 18). In providing something of a definition, the *Directory* states: 'In the realm of pastoral activity, catechesis is that ecclesial activity which leads the community and individual Christians to maturity of faith. With the help of catechesis, Christian communities acquire a more profound knowledge of God and of his salvation, centred on Christ, Word of God incarnate; they develop by endeavouring to make their faith mature and enlightened . . .' (n. 21).

Many more important statements about catechesis are made throughout the document. Catechesis must encourage people to take on the responsibilities of their faith, particularly in relation to others; it is not just about stimulating a religious experience, but it should contribute to the gradual grasping of the whole truth of faith; it should promote an active, conscious, genuine participation in the liturgy of the Church, forming people for prayer, thanksgiving and a true liturgical life; it must also train people to meditate on the Word of God and engage in private prayer; it should help people to interpret the signs of the times in a Christian spirit; it should assist in the journey towards Christian unity and help to spread the light of the gospel; it acknowledges the different stages that people might be at in the life of faith and performs the functions of initiation, education and formation.

The Church was clearly taking on board the challenge of proclaiming the gospel in the modern world. In the light of this, the *Directory* called for a double fidelity to the Word of God and to the reality of the human situation:

> Catechesis derives the truth from the word of God, totally committed to its security when it is given expression, and it endeavours to teach this word of God in total fidelity. However, the task cannot be merely a matter of repeating traditional formulas. The formulas must be understood and, where necessary, faithfully re-formulated in language suited to the capacity of the audience. The language will be different for different age groups, social conditions, cultures and civilisations. (n. 34)

REFLECTION

- 'The catechist is, as it were, the interpreter of the Church for those who are to be catechised. He reads the signs of the faith, of which the Church is the chief one, and teaches how they should be read' (n. 35). How challenging is this? Do you feel excited by such a challenge or see such an approach as full of fear?

- 'No method, however well proven by experience, exempts the catechist from the task of personally weighing and judging the concrete situation and adjusting to it. Excellent human and Christian qualities in catechists are a greater guarantee of success than the methods chosen. The work of the catechist must be considered of greater importance than the choice of texts and of other work tools' (n. 71). What sort of responsibilities does this put on the catechist? What does this say about his or her vocation?

- 'The content of catechesis is to be found in the word of
  God in scripture and tradition; its meaning is more deeply
  penetrated and developed by the community of believers
  under the guidance of the magisterium, the sole authentic
  teacher; it is celebrated in liturgy; it shines out in the life of
  the Church, especially in the holy people and in saints; and
  to some extent it appears in the genuine moral values which
  by God's providence exist in society' (n. 45). How helpful is
  this vision to the work of the catechist? Does it offer a plan
  or structure which can be adapted to parish catechesis?

The Christian message

The *General Catechetical Directory* went on to talk about the
content of the Christian message, pointing out the link between
the faith *by which* one believes and the faith *which* one believes.
The former is a personal relationship with God, unique to each
individual, while the latter is the content of that faith. In setting
out the content of faith, the *Directory* did not set out to be
prescriptive but simply referred to what it called 'some of the
more outstanding elements contained in the saving message . . .
especially in those particular features which must be brought
out more clearly in a new, adapted catechesis which pursues
its goal faithfully' (n. 36).

Some might see this as a subtle return to a doctrine-led
catechesis, but this was clearly not the aim of the *Directory*. Nor
was this an attempt to point out what might have been perceived as previous errors in catechetical theory and practice.
Rather, the *Directory* was trying to get across the point that faith
is a whole and not just a selection of different doctrines:

> Since the purpose of catechesis . . . consists in leading indi-
> vidual Christians and communities to a mature faith, it
> must take diligent care faithfully to present the entire
> treasure of the Christian message . . . Catechesis begins,
> therefore, with a rather simple presentation of the entire
> structure of the Christian message (using also summary or
> global formulas), and it presents this in a way appropriate

to the various cultural and spiritual conditions of those to
be taught. (n. 38)

Part Four of the *General Catechetical Directory* is devoted to
methodology, the 'how' of handing on faith. One of the clearest,
and perhaps boldest, statements is made at the start of this
section: 'The work of the catechist must be considered of greater
importance than the selection of texts and other tools' (n. 71).
It is the personal witness, not the value of a particular text,
which lies at the heart of catechesis. The best tool for handing
on faith is a person, not a book.

The methods which that person might use can be varied. The
Directory speaks of the usefulness of formulae ('suitable for
correct exposition of the faith', n. 73), but balances such an
approach with some important comments on experience. This
latter 'gives rise to concern and questioning, hope and anxiety,
reflection and judgement' (n. 74); experience can make us
respond to God but can also help make the Christian message
more intelligible, just as Christ himself preached the kingdom
of God by illustrating its nature with parables drawn from the
experiences of human life; and finally, experience 'needs to be
illuminated by the light of revelation. Catechesis, by recalling
the work of God in effecting salvation, should help people to
examine, interpret and judge their experiences and to give a
Christian meaning to their own existence' (n. 74).

In some respects, these brief comments on experience
reflected a debate which is still going on in catechesis today.
This debate, which centres around the role of experience in
catechesis, can be summed up quite simply: should catechesis
begin with experience and let this be enlightened by the
Christian message, or should the Christian message, which is
then brought to bear on experience, be the starting-point? The
Directory acknowledged the value of both the inductive and
deductive methods of catechesis. Irrespective of the method
used, catechesis must stimulate activity or creativity. It is 'active
education', since it is looking for an active response to God's
call.

The rest of the *General Catechetical Directory* went on to make
points that might seem obvious to the reader of a text published

more than thirty years ago. But at the time, and in an official document of this type, the statements were of great importance. Part Five, 'Catechesis By Age Level', insisted that catechesis reflect the age and stage of faith development of the hearers. Here is an acknowledgement that faith grows and develops throughout life, with great emphasis on catechesis of adults. Part Six, entitled 'Pastoral Action, The Ministry of the Word', is essentially about resources. Every Bishops' Conference is called upon to establish an episcopal commission for catechesis, while at diocesan level there should be higher institutes for training in pastoral catechetics or schools of religious education. Reference is also made to national or local catechetical directories and catechisms. The purpose of catechisms

> is to convey in summary and practical form the documents of revelation and of Christian tradition, as well as the main elements which must be of service for catechetical activity, that is, for personal education in faith. The documents of tradition ought therefore to be held in proper esteem and the greatest care is to be taken lest particular interpretations, which are only private opinions or the opinions of some theological school, be presented as the teachings of faith. (n. 119)

As regards manuals for catechists, the *Directory* makes it clear that these are not just reference books of doctrinal content but works which must also contain psychological and pedagogical advice and suggestions about methods.

The *General Catechetical Directory* ends with an Appendix dealing with the controversial subject of the first reception of the sacraments of penance and Eucharist. It is included because of 'some experiments that have been taking place recently in some parts of the Church' (Appendix, n. 1). In practical terms it is a reminder that the age for receiving these sacraments is the age of reason, which is said to be about age seven, and the order for these sacraments – penance followed by Eucharist – does not need to be changed (although it does not rule out changes where permission is properly sought and deemed fit). With this in mind, the Appendix speaks of the important work of proper catechesis in this delicate area.

The importance of the *General Catechetical Directory* cannot be underestimated. It was a groundbreaking document. In North America alone, 75,000 copies of the English translation were distributed within a year of its publication. The emphasis in catechetics had shifted from content to guidelines, on the 'how' of handing on faith. Uniformity was no longer a central theme, the local authority of bishops was recognised and the *Directory* encouraged the publication of national and regional documents. More than thirty years later it is still seen as reflecting a sea-change in catechetics. Faith is no longer equated with intellectual knowledge, and so catechetics can no longer be equated with 'catechism'.

REFLECTION

- 'The summit and centre of catechetical formation consists in the aptitude and the ability to communicate the gospel message' (*GCD*, n. 111). What do you think 'aptitude' and 'ability' mean in this context?
- 'Catechists need a preparation that will fit them to interpret accurately the reactions of a group or of an individual, to discern their spiritual aptitude and to choose the method that will enable the gospel message to be heard fruitfully and effectively' (n. 113). How could a catechist be prepared for such a task? Why is such discernment important?
- 'The catechists' task demands an intense sacramental and spiritual life, a habit of prayer, a profound sense of the pre-eminence of the Christian message and of its ability to transform people's lives. It also requires the cultivation of charity, humility and prudence, which permit the Holy Spirit to complete his fruitful labours in those being catechised' (n. 114). What picture of the catechist does this paint? Can you discern some essential characteristics of the catechist?
- The *General Catechetical Directory* spoke of the catechesis of adults as the 'principal kind of catechesis, towards which all other forms, while always needed, are directed' (n. 20). What do you think this means? How important and relevant is it?
- 'The heart of modern catechetics is teaching from life . . . [The

Directory] suggests that only our Lord's methods of religious instruction are sound. It is not surprising that after twenty centuries we should re-discover the fact that Christ understood better than anyone the best way to teach religion'.[3] Any comment?

Responses to the General Catechetical Directory

Five months after the publication of the *General Catechetical Directory*, Rome hosted an International Catechetical Congress. At its conclusion, Archbishop Knox of Melbourne read a statement which eventually made its way into the formal conclusions of the Congress:

> The Delegates of the Congress are appreciative of the spirit and intention in which the *Directorium Catechisticum Generale* has been published. As Cardinal Wright [Prefect of the Sacred Congregation for the Clergy] declared to the press: 'The basic purpose of the Directory is to provide an orientation for religious formation, rather than to establish binding rules'. It contains updated orientational guidelines rather than prescriptions. The Directory will serve as a basic document meant to be adapted to local cultural and pastoral situations of each country under the guidance of the local Episcopal Conference in consultation with the Holy See.

By the time the *General Catechetical Directory* was published, many Bishops' Conferences throughout the world had begun to reflect on the broader issues of education and formation and the problems of proclaiming the gospel in the modern world. The fruit of their deliberations and consultations was seen in a number of documents that appeared during the 'Decade of Directories'.

In 1972, in the United States, the National Conference of Catholic Bishops (NCCB) published a pastoral document on Catholic education, *To Teach As Jesus Did*. Although sections of the document are addressed specifically to the world of 'Higher Education', 'Campus Ministry', and 'The Educational Ministry to Youth', some general statements are worthy of note. The bishops state that

> Catholic education is an expression of the mission entrusted by Jesus to the Church He founded. Through education the Church seeks to prepare its members to proclaim the Good News and to translate this proclamation into action. (n. 7) . . . one crucial measure of the success or failure of the educational ministry is how well it enables men to hear the message of hope contained in the Gospel, to base their love and service of God upon this message, to achieve a vital personal relationship with Christ, and to share the Gospel's realistic view of the human condition which recognizes the fact of evil and personal sin while affirming hope. (n. 8)

The clear message is one of faith into action. All catechesis is about translating faith into action, so that it impacts upon daily life. What is believed must make a difference to daily life. As the American bishops stated further on in this document '. . . doctrine is not merely a matter for the intellect, but is the basis for a way of life'.

To Teach As Jesus Did was followed a year later by another American bishops' document, *Basic Teachings For Catholic Religious Education*. This was closely connected to the *General Catechetical Directory* and in fact mirrored some of the contents of that document. Some of the points raised by *Basic Teachings For Catholic Religious Education* are still worth reflecting on today. The Introduction states that all religious education 'is formation in Christ, given to make "faith become living, conscious and active, through the light of instruction". Religious education is proclaiming to others the Gospel of the risen Lord, while showing that this "Good News" alone gives meaning to life'. But it goes on: 'No list of documents can bring about real religious education, but certain basic teachings are necessary for doctrinal substance and stability'.

Here was a clear reminder that faith must be a lived thing, not just a matter of referring to documents. There is a balance, however, for there are doctrinal truths which must be understood, offering 'substance and stability'. In subsequent years, this idea would be expressed as the 'Catholic literacy' which must be handed on with faith. The American bishops also used an inspirational quote from a series of lectures given by John Henry Cardinal Newman (1801–90) in 1852 entitled *Present Position of Catholics in England*, describing the knowledge of religion expected in his day: 'We want a laity . . . who know their religion, who enter into it, who know just where they stand, who know what they hold and what they do not, who know their creed so well that they can give an account of it, who know so much history that they can defend it'. And the American bishops go on:

> A century later, the Bishops want all this. But they ask and pray for much more – for a laity transformed by the Gospel message, who put the Gospel to work in every action of their daily lives, whose joy and simplicity and concern for others are so radiant that all men recognize them as Christ's disciples by the love they have for one another.

This remains the challenge of catechesis today.

The catechetical picture was also developing rapidly in England and Wales. Just two years after the *General Catechetical Directory*, the bishops of England and Wales published an Australian translation of the Italian bishops' document *Il rinnovamento della catechesi*, giving it the title *Teaching the Faith 'the New Way'*. The wording used in the titles is revealing. The document published by the Italian bishops in 1970 is translated literally 'The renewal of catechesis'; the Australian bishops' translation was published as *The Renewal of the Education of Faith*; and in England and Wales the same text was published as *Teaching the Faith 'the New Way'*. In a subtle way 'catechesis' in the original had become 'the education of faith' and then 'teaching the new way'. While 'catechesis' maintains all the implications of development and process, 'teaching' returns to a more authoritarian tone, a more disciplined approach.

The Synod of Bishops

After the Second Vatican Council, Pope Paul VI established the Synod of Bishops, a consultative body to meet in Rome every three years. In 1974 the Synod met to discuss evangelisation and three years later catechetics was the chosen theme. The work of these two Synods closely reflected the work of the Council and was carried out in the context that we have just seen with regard to evangelisation and catechetics at a local level, at a time when national catechetical documents were being published in different parts of the world.

The fruit of the 1974 Synod of Bishops was Pope Paul VI's document *On Evangelization in the Modern World*, promulgated on 8 December 1975 exactly ten years after the end of the Council. He posed the question: 'after the Council and thanks to the Council, which was a time given her by God, at this turning-point of history, does the Church or does she not find herself better equipped to proclaim the Gospel and to put it into people's hearts with conviction, freedom of spirit and effectiveness?'[4]

Some commentators see this document as one of the most important issued since the Second Vatican Council. Pope Paul VI stressed that evangelisation is the essential mission of the Church and everything within the Church must be geared to proclaiming the Good News. He wrote,

> For the Church evangelizing means bringing the Good News into all the strata of humanity, and through its influence transforming humanity from within and making it new ... But there is no new humanity if there are not first of all new persons renewed by Baptism and by lives lived according to the Gospel. The purpose of evangelization is therefore precisely this interior change, and if it had to be expressed in one sentence the best way of stating it would be to say that the Church evangelizes when she seeks to convert, solely through the divine power of the Message she proclaims, both the personal and collective consciences of people, the activities in which they engage, and the lives and concrete milieus which are theirs.[5]

Many of the themes and statements contained in *On Evangelization in the Modern World* have strong echoes in catechetics, too.
Indeed, one of the effects of this document was to show how
closely these two topics – evangelisation and catechetics – are
interlinked. Pope Paul VI stressed the importance of the evan-
geliser and the key role that is assigned to their apostolate:
' . . . the person who has been evangelized goes on to evangelize
others. Here lies the test of truth, the touchstone of evangelization: it is unthinkable that a person should accept the Word
and give himself to the Kingdom without becoming a person
who bears witness to it and proclaims it in his turn'.[6] And in two
passages often quoted by the late Archbishop of Westminster,
Cardinal George Basil Hume (1923–99): 'Modern man listens
more willingly to witnesses than to teachers, and if he does
listen to teachers, it is because they are witnesses'[7] and ' . . . the
world is calling for evangelizers to speak to it of a God whom
the evangelists themselves should know and be familiar with
as if they could see the invisible'.[8]

In *On Evangelization in the Modern World* the Pope also speaks
of the twofold fidelity to the message proclaimed and to the
recipients of that message. Indeed, the Pope declares that 'evangelization would not be complete if it did not take account of
the unceasing interplay of the Gospel and of man's concrete life,
both personal and social. This is why evangelization evolves an
explicit message adapted to the different situations constantly
being realized . . .'[9]

In talking about how to evangelise, Pope Paul VI devotes a
small section to catechetics, a 'means of evangelization that
must not be neglected' (n. 44). The line of thought is very clear:

> No one will deny that this instruction must be given to
> form patterns of Christian living and not to remain only
> notional . . . The methods [of teaching] must be adapted to
> the age, culture and aptitude of the persons concerned;
> they must seek always to fix in the memory, intelligence
> and heart the essential truths that must impregnate all of
> life. It is necessary above all to prepare good instructors –
> parochial catechists, teachers, parents – who are desirous

of perfecting themselves in this superior art, which is indispensable and requires religious instruction.[10]

Catechesis in our Time

In October 1977, the Synod of Bishops met once again in Rome, this time with catechesis as their theme, with particular reference to children and young people. The month-long meeting ended with a Message from the Bishops to the People of God and a set of thirty-four resolutions from the bishops presented to Pope Paul VI. But within a year, both Pope Paul VI and his successor, Pope John Paul I, the oft-called 'smiling Pope', had died. On 16 October 1978 the pontificate of John Paul II commenced. Exactly one year later, on 16 October 1979, he issued his document on the 1977 Synod entitled *Catechesis in our Time*. In the Introduction, Pope John Paul II states that his purpose here is to continue the work already begun by Pope Paul VI with the documents from the Synod. He goes on:

> Pope John Paul I, whose zeal and gifts as a catechist amazed us all, had taken them in hand and was preparing to publish them when he was suddenly called to God. To all of us he gave an example of catechesis at once popular and concentrated on the essential, one made up of simple words and actions that were able to touch the heart. (n. 4)

Just as Pope Paul VI had placed evangelisation at the heart of the Church's mission, so Pope John Paul II roots catechesis among the primary tasks of the Church: ' ... the name of catechesis was given to the whole of the efforts within the Church to make disciples, to help people believe that Jesus is the Son of God, so that believing they might have life in his name, and to educate and instruct them in this life and thus build up the Body of Christ'.[11]

But Pope John Paul II was quick to set down what could be called, in an echo of Pope Paul VI's phrase about evangelisation, the 'touchstone of catechesis', the Christocentricity of all authentic catechesis. At the heart of catechesis is a Person, Jesus of Nazareth, the essential object of catechesis. Christocentricity in

catechesis 'also means the intention to transmit not one's own
teaching or that of some other master, but the teaching of
Jesus Christ, the Truth that he communicates or, to put it more
precisely, the Truth that he is'.[12] Catechesis is not about personal
opinions and options: 'Every catechist should be able to apply
to himself the mysterious words of Jesus: "My teaching is not
mine, but his who sent me" '.[13] Some may have interpreted this
as a critical reaction to the way catechesis had developed. Pope
John Paul II was stating quite clearly that the centre of attention
in catechesis is Jesus Christ, not the catechist. In this, he was
perhaps reflecting some of the discussion that had gone on
during the Synod, when many tensions and controversies were
aired. The final document speaks of the need for balance in
catechesis, finding a path which is neither routine ('with its
refusal to accept any change' n. 17) nor improvisation ('with
its readiness for any ventures' n. 17).

Catechesis remains, however, at the heart of the Church's
pastoral activity.

> The more the Church, whether on the local or the universal
> level, gives catechesis priority over other works and under-
> takings the results of which would be more spectacular,
> the more she finds in catechesis a strengthening of her
> internal life as a community of believers and of her external
> activity as a missionary Church. As the twentieth century
> draws to a close, the Church is bidden by God and by
> events – each of them a call from him – to renew her trust
> in catechetical activity as a prime aspect of her mission.[14]

Pope John Paul II even goes on to say that the Church's 'best
resources in people and energy, without sparing effort, toil or
material means' should be devoted to catechesis. 'This is no
mere human calculation,' he wrote, 'it is an attitude of faith'
(n. 15). If that was the mandate in 1979, an audit today could
be an interesting exercise!

The titles of other sections of *Catechesis in our Time* paint an
interesting picture of the vision and direction which the Church
was offering for catechesis: 'Catechesis in the Church's Pastoral
and Missionary Activity', 'The Whole of the Good News Drawn
From Its Source', 'Everybody Needs to be Catechized', 'Some

Ways and Means of Catechesis', 'How to Impart Catechesis', 'The Joy of Faith in a Troubled World', and 'The Task Concerns Us All'. Catechesis is very firmly rooted within the Church and it is the task of everyone within the Church. In more formal language, catechesis is both christocentric and ecclesial. *Catechesis in our Time* also reflects the growing development of the link between catechesis and evangelisation, which had begun with the Second Vatican Council when the Church began to look more beyond itself to the outside world.

In fact, Pope John Paul II noted that catechesis is a stage in evangelisation. He referred to catechesis as 'an education of children, young people and adults in the faith, which includes especially the teaching of Christian doctrine imparted, generally speaking, in an organic and systematic way, with a view to initiating the hearers into the fullness of Christian life'.[15] The Pope said there was no separation or opposition between catechesis and evangelisation, nor can they be identified with each other, but they integrate and complement each other.

One of the important words used here in relation to catechesis is 'systematic'. At the Synod, the bishops had spoken of the ongoing tension between doctrine and life-experience, particularly in conjunction with the methods to be used in catechesis. In *Catechesis in our Time* the Pope attempts to iron out some of these practical difficulties, by stating that instruction

> must be systematic, not improvised but programmed to reach a precise goal; it must deal with essentials, without any claim to tackle all disputed questions or to transform itself into theological research or scientific exegesis; it must nevertheless be sufficiently complete, not stopping short at the initial proclamation of the Christian mystery such as we have in the *kerygma*; it must be an integral Christian initiation, open to all the other factors of Christian life . . . I am stressing the need for organic and systematic Christian instruction, because of the tendency in various quarters to minimize its importance.[16]

The implication is clear. The doctrinal content of catechesis is not to be minimalised. It cannot be replaced simply by reflections on life-experience. *Catechesis in our Time* is quite blunt on this point, but calls for the balance which to this day reflects one of the great challenges in the catechetical world:

> It is also quite useless to campaign for the abandonment of serious and orderly study of the message of Christ in the name of a method concentrating on life experience . . . Nor is any opposition to be set up between a catechesis taking life as its point of departure and a traditional, doctrinal and systematic catechesis. Authentic catechesis is always an orderly and systematic initiation into the revelation that God has given of himself to humanity in Christ Jesus, a revelation stored in the depths of the Church's memory and in Sacred Scripture, and constantly communicated from one generation to the next by a living active *traditio*. This revelation is not however isolated from life or artificially juxtaposed to it. It is concerned with the ultimate meaning of life and it illumines the whole of life with the light of the Gospel, to inspire it or to question it.[17]

The language used here might seem quite guarded, but it clearly reflects the tensions experienced by the bishops in the late 1970s. Pope John Paul II was clearly not stifling development, but was keen to acknowledge the reality of those tensions and attempt a solution that would not resort to the adopting of extreme, opposing positions.[18] Catechesis was no longer seen as the simple teaching of the formulae that express faith, but was aimed at the maturing of that faith as a support to witnessing to it in the world.

Like preceding documents, *Catechesis in our Time* acknowledged the need for different methods to be used in education in the faith. However, Pope John Paul II warned against the

> danger and the temptation to mix catechetical teaching unduly with overt or masked ideological views, especially political and social ones, or with personal political options. When such views get the better of the central message to be transmitted, to the point of obscuring it and putting it in second place or even using it to further their own ends, catechesis then becomes radically distorted.[19]

Catechesis is called 'to bring the power of the Gospel into

the very heart of culture and cultures', the Pope wrote (n. 53). However, inculturation, too, has its parameters, for 'the Gospel message cannot be purely and simply isolated from the culture in which it was first inserted ... nor, without serious loss, from the cultures in which it has already been expressed down the centuries ... There would be no catechesis if it were the Gospel that had to change when it came into contact with the cultures'.[20] In further comments concerning the methodology to be used in catechesis, Pope John Paul II referred to the contribution of popular devotions ('even if the faith underlining them needs to be purified or rectified in many aspects', n. 54), and the traditional catechetical tool of memorising texts. He noted that at the Synod some bishops had called for 'the restoration of a judicious balance between reflection and spontaneity, between dialogue and silence, between written work and memory work' (n. 55). The Pope's heartfelt plea is clear:

> We must be realists. The blossoms, if we may call them that, of faith and piety do not grow in the desert places of a memory-less catechesis. What is essential is that the texts that are memorized must at the same time be taken in and gradually understood in depth, in order to become a source of Christian life on the personal level and community level.[21]

And, concluding his thoughts on methodology in catechesis, he continues:

> The plurality of methods in contemporary catechesis can be a sign of vitality and ingenuity. In any case, the method chosen must ultimately be referred to a law that is fundamental for the whole of the Church's life: the law of fidelity to God and fidelity to man in a single loving attitude.[22]

Once again, the Pope is calling for a careful balance in catechesis, an idea that is repeated in his comments on language suited to the handing on of faith:

> For catechesis has a pressing obligation to speak a language suited to today's children and young people in general and to many other categories of people – the language of

students, intellectuals and scientists; the language of the illiterate or of people of simple culture; the language of the handicapped, and so on ... but there is good reason for recalling here that catechesis cannot admit any language that would result in altering the substance of the content of the Creed, under any pretext whatever, even a pretended scientific one. Deceitful or beguiling language is no better. On the contrary, the supreme rule is that the great advances in the science of language must be capable of being placed at the service of catechesis so as to enable it really to 'tell' or 'communicate' to the child, the adolescent, the young people and adults of today the whole content of doctrine without distortion.[23]

What a challenge for handing on faith in an intelligible manner.

REFLECTION

• Talking about the method to be used in evangelisation, Pope Paul VI urges that 'the content of evangelization must not overshadow the importance of the ways and means'.[24] How does this careful remark about the balance between content and method strike you?

• *Catechesis in our Time* states that the bishop must 'let the concern to foster active and effective catechesis yield to no other care whatever in any way. This concern will lead you to transmit personally to your faithful the doctrine of life'.[25] How realistic is this? How can the bishop make catechesis his primary concern?

• ' ... the parish community must continue to be the prime mover and pre-eminent place for catechesis'.[26] How? In what different areas of parish life does catechesis take place?

• What do you think are the particular challenges for handing on faith in the family and in school? Are these two environments isolated? Do they call for specific support? Who is responsible for catechesis in these places?

• Both *On Evangelization in the Modern World* and *Catechesis in our Time* spoke of the need for faithfulness to the world and

faithfulness to the Church. Is this realistic? How might this
be possible?

4 R.C.I.A. – Rite of Christian Initiation of Adults . . . *or* *'Roman Catholics in Agony'*?

After the Second Vatican Council, it was clear that many things in the Church would never be the same again. Although the most visible example of change was the language used in the celebration of Mass – no longer Latin but the vernacular – this was really the tip of the iceberg. The fundamental process of 'becoming a Catholic' was also to change dramatically in the years following the Council.

Historically, we have seen that, as one author put it, from 'the sixth to the sixteenth century the Western Church went into a great sleep as far as new membership was concerned'.[1] What evangelising efforts were made were focused on the Americas, as missionaries went out to convert the pagans. There was little structure to this work, and the emphasis was more on salvation through baptism than formation for a Christian way of life – compared to the early centuries when Christian formation was a prerequisite *before* baptism. In subsequent centuries, attention turned to the Far East and then to Africa, and it was from Africa, in the years before the Second Vatican Council, that the call came for a clear structure for bringing new members into the Church. At the Council, the bishops heeded that call: 'The catechumenate for adults, divided into several distinct steps, is to be restored and brought into use at the discretion of the local Ordinary. By this means, the time of the catechumenate, which is destined for the requisite formation, may be sanctified by sacred rites to be celebrated at successive stages'.[2]

The impact of this short paragraph from the *Constitution on the Sacred Liturgy* needs to be put into a clear context for it to be understood. Prior to this, 'becoming', or, to use a popular phrase, 'turning Catholic' was a very private affair. Adults received private instruction from the parish priest on a one-to-one basis. After some time, the priest would decide that the person was ready to become a Catholic and they would be baptised in a private ceremony. There are stories of priests telephoning 'good parishioners' and asking them to come to church at a certain time so that that they could witness the baptism of an adult who had just finished instruction. In some cases friends or family might be present, but it was clear they were attending a 'private' function. After this, the 'new' Catholic joined the community at worship, no fuss, no ceremony, and no further means of helping them to settle into that community and way of life. Instruction was complete.

Such a way of doing things was about to be turned on its head. The catechumenate, as it had flourished between the second and fifth centuries, was to be restored. Within three years of the Council Fathers' call for the restoration of the catechumenate, provisional texts were distributed. After comments on these were returned and amendments made, a second text was distributed for experimental use (1969). The official Latin text, the *Ordo initiationis christianae adultorum*, was promulgated on 6 January 1972. The official English translation, the *Rite of Christian Initiation of Adults* (RCIA), appeared in 1974.

The changes were dramatic. What was on offer was not just a new Rite, but a new model that was to be the definitive model for *all* catechesis, from children through to adults. The initiation of adults into the Church was no longer something private, but a public journey in the midst of the community. Words like 'conversion' and 'turning Catholic' were replaced by 'initiation' and 'journey of faith'. Conversion was not a one-off event, but the RCIA implied the daily conversions that all Christians need to undertake in responding to God. Candidates no longer went on a course of instruction which offered information, but began a *process* that had no set timescale. When someone became a Catholic no longer depended on the parish priest's decision that enough information had been imparted and assimilated, but when a candidate, working at his/her own pace, felt comfortable enough in the stage of the journey. And that person was not the only one on the journey. There might be other people in a group, some might already be Catholics, but all are on a journey of faith, a journey of continual conversion. It was partly this dramatic change, encapsulated in the phrase 'from instruction in the faith to process', that was later to make some critics of the RCIA refer to it as 'Roman Catholics in Agony'. The tensions in the world of catechetics were still present.

REFLECTION

• Do you remember anything about people 'becoming Catholic' before the advent of the RCIA? What are their stories?
• What are the advantages of 'instruction' on a private, one-to-one basis? What are the disadvantages?
• What sort of role might there be for the community in 'handing on faith' or helping people to become new members of the Church? Or is it primarily, or even exclusively, the priest's role?

So just what is the RCIA?

The introduction of the *Rite of Christian Initiation of Adults* set down many new markers in terms of catechesis. Principally, these were to do with both the individual and the community. As noted before, becoming a new member of the Church had, in the past, largely involved instruction given by the parish priest. Now, in a sense, the pace of the journey of faith – to use the language of a process in and towards faith – is dictated by the individual. The process acknowledges the faith development of the individual, being formed in the faith within a living community. It is formation within a community, not information imparted within a one-to-one teaching environment. There is a clear role, then, for the community, which is travelling on the journey along with those interested in joining it. The faithful must use the opportunity offered by the RCIA to reflect on their own faith and their own daily conversion. 'A parish community discovers itself when it gathers to initiate new members. I cannot welcome the new without asking what it means to already be'.[3]

At the heart of the RCIA is a gradual process of initiation

identified through four stages, each marked by a distinctive rite or celebration within the parish community. Each rite marks a new stage in the journey of faith, the journey of conversion. The four stages are: Evangelization and the Pre-catechumenate, the Catechumenate, Purification and Enlightenment, and finally Mystagogy (Period of Post-baptismal Catechesis).

The first stage is a period of 'inquiry', or, as it is called in the official text, Evangelization and the Pre-Catechumenate. This is a time of no fixed duration for 'inquirers', those who, for whatever reason, may be interested in reflecting upon their faith. Each individual enters upon this stage for his or her own personal reason. Some parishes advertise in the local media, offering 'Talks on the Catholic Faith' to which all are invited; more often, individuals may be responding to a particular experience or to meeting a particular individual. This may have stimulated within them a need to inquire, to seek more. In this context, this is what evangelisation means: it is not a response to a 'fundamental' proclamation of the gospel imposed from the outside, but a response to a simple witness to living out the gospel in daily life. It is often that which prompts people to 'inquire' more. This is the period of inquiry, a time when basic questions can be answered, and a basic understanding and feeling for the Christian faith, as expressed according to the Catholic tradition, can be experienced. Although it is not directly to be compared to the era of private instruction, the inquiry period can often be largely 'informational' in providing answers to particular questions. This time is also called the 'Pre-catechumenate' because at the end of this period the inquirer may decide to be enrolled into the catechumenate.

This whole process, this journey of faith, is regularly marked by rites (hence the name *Rite of Christian Initiation of Adults*), liturgical celebrations marking the different stages of the journey. And so, if an inquirer decides to proceed along the journey of faith in this formal sense (and it is important that this be a free choice), there is a rite to mark the acceptance into the Order of the Catechumens, the second stage of the RCIA.

The catechumenate is a period of formation, building upon

the period of information. It is formation through catechesis and liturgy, leading the catechumens

> not only to an appropriate acquaintance with dogmas and precepts but also to a profound sense of the mystery of salvation in which they desire to participate. As they become familiar with the Christian way of life and are helped by the example and support of sponsors, god-parents, and the entire Christian community, the catechumens learn to turn more readily to God in prayer, to bear witness to the faith, in all things to keep their hopes set on Christ, to follow supernatural inspiration in their deeds, and to practise love of neighbour ... Thus formed, the newly converted set out on a spiritual journey. Already sharing through faith in the mystery of Christ's death and resurrection, they pass from the old to a new nature made perfect in Christ. Since this transition brings with it a pro-gressive change of outlook and conduct, it should become manifest by means of its social consequences and it should develop gradually during the period of the catechumenate.[4]

Already, one can detect the links with the catechumenate of the early centuries, which set great store by the need for a change of lifestyle for those who wished to become Christians. The Word of God was not something to be taken lightly, for adherence to it had important consequences in daily life. The RCIA talks of the 'social consequences' of the catechumenate. Today, this period of the process is very much based on the Lectionary, the daily readings which run throughout the Church's year. The connection with the catechumenate is made even more explicit by the suggestion that the catechumens, when present in the assembly of the faithful, 'should be kindly dismissed before the liturgy of the eucharist begins ... For they must await baptism, which will join them to God's priestly people and empower them to participate in Christ's worship'.[5] The idea behind this dismissal of the catechumens is simple. Ideally, they are invited to go with their catechist and 'break the Word of God' together; at this stage in their journey of faith they cannot share fully the breaking of the bread with the community, but they can share the breaking of the Word. What they share with the community is the Word, not the fullness of the Eucharist. This division between the Word and Eucharist in the situation of a typical weekend parish liturgy might seem idealistic. However, the sign it gives is, I believe, very powerful. The Word of God unites us. But the catechumens do not, as yet, share the fullness of the Eucharist. Their nourishment is the Word of God. Of course, a technical difference arises between those who are catechumens (i.e., not baptised) and those who are candidates (i.e., already baptised). A high degree of pastoral sensitivity needs to be exercised here. There is something to be said for candidates being part of the catechumenate, since this latter must be understood as formation in its broadest sense, and those who are already baptised have something to contribute from their own experience, which should not be lost by placing them in a different category.

Above all, it is perhaps the catechumenate which today reflects the early Church's preoccupation with the need to be absolutely sure that someone wanted to become a Christian. The length of the catechumenate is indeterminate. And, as has been noted before, the leading player here is no longer the priest, but the candidate. Gone is the notion of a set programme, at the end of which one is able to become a Catholic because enough information has been imparted. It is a journey, not a programme, and it is a journey on which the candidate must feel comfortable and at home. Hence, the length of the catechumenate is not a problem. A catechumen may need any amount of time – and here reference can be made to years rather than months – before feeling ready to take the next step on the journey of faith, before feeling ready to make that further commitment to Jesus Christ. Indeed, such a time-span often presents challenges to people who have been Catholics from birth (occasionally referred to by the horrible phrase 'cradle Catholics'), and may have not thought so deeply about what that means in terms of commitment. They see people around them taking a number of months or years to think about what it really means each day to be a disciple of Jesus Christ, and it can be quite a thought-provoking experience.

Just as a person may decide to move from inquiry to catechumenate, so another decision is taken to move – or not – to the third stage of the RCIA, the Period of Purification and Enlightenment. The catechumenate closes with a special rite called the 'Rite of Election'. This usually coincides with the start of Lent and is celebrated in cathedral churches on the First Sunday of Lent in the presence of the bishop or his delegate. The catechumenate has been a lengthy period of formation of the catechumens' 'minds and hearts'; the Rite of Election 'also marks the beginning of the period of final, more intense preparation for the sacraments of initiation, during which the elect will be encouraged to follow Christ with greater generosity'.[6] This is a clear return to the early Christian period of intense preparation during the season of Lent. In the terminology of the RCIA, the decision to move forward along this journey of faith means that the catechumens have now become the 'elect'. Of course, this is not a term used with any suggestion of superiority or elitism, but is rooted in the Latin word *electio*, meaning 'a choice', referring to a catechumen

> chosen by God through the community of faith to take part in the next celebration of the Sacraments of Initiation;[7]
>
> . . . on the basis of the testimony of godparents and catechists and of the catechumens' reaffirmation of their intention, the Church judges their state of readiness and decides on their advancement towards the sacraments of initiation. Thus the Church makes its 'election', that is, the choice and admission of those catechumens who have the dispositions that make them fit to take part, at the next major celebration, in the sacraments of initiation.[8]

This period of purification and enlightenment is often likened to an intensive personal retreat. This point is made clear by the *Rite of Christian Initiation of Adults* itself, which notes that this period is one of 'more intense spiritual preparation, consisting more in interior reflection than in catechetical instruction, and is intended to purify the minds and hearts of the elect as they search their own consciences and do penance. This period is intended as well to enlighten the minds and hearts of the elect with a deeper knowledge of Christ the Saviour'.[9]

The period of purification and enlightenment is focused on

celebrating the sacraments of initiation at Easter. This is the next stage in the Christian initiation of adults, usually celebrated at the Easter Vigil. At the Easter Vigil we witness one of the major developments brought about by the RCIA: new members are welcomed into the Christian community in the presence of the community, not in some private ceremony. The role of the community is clear, supporting the candidates by presence, prayer and witness.

But that is not the end of the journey. More importantly, it should not be the end of the support for the new members of the Christian community. Whereas in the past 'instruction' may have ended when someone became a Catholic and was immersed – maybe to sink or swim – in an altogether new way of life, the RCIA offers yet another stage on the journey of faith, which bears the title Period of Post-baptismal Catechesis or Mystagogy. As mentioned already, the word 'mystagogy' has its roots in the Greek words *mystes*, an initiate, and *agein*, to lead. There is also a return to the early Christian terminology for the newly-baptised who, as seen earlier, were known as 'neophytes' (rooted in the Greek *neos*, meaning 'new', and *phutos*, 'grown'; *neophutos* means 'newly planted').

The period of post-baptismal catechesis is perhaps one of the most challenging in many parishes today. The RCIA rightly calls for the process of the journey of faith to continue *after* the celebration of the sacraments of initiation. Yet there may be a temptation to see these sacraments as a point of arrival rather than a point of departure, or, even worse, to see initiation in modern-day consumer terms of purchasing a commodity. Indeed, for all those truly professing some sort of belief there must be a step away from any view which sees faith in terms of a 'checklist mentality', as in 'Been there, done that, bought the T-shirt'. If belief is truly held, then it must make a difference in daily life, as seen by the early Christians' idea that certain professions were incompatible with Christian life and could not be continued if one were serious about becoming a Christian.

The period of post-baptismal catechesis, then, offers an important challenge to the community that, at the Easter Vigil, has rejoiced in the new members joining it. To put it simply: do parishes, faithful to the RCIA, continue the journey with those who have celebrated the sacraments of initiation? What do parishes do to ensure that new members of the community are supported in their new way of faith and life? For this is what the text of the *Rite of Christian Initiation of Adults* declares about the period of mystagogy:

> This is a time for the community and the neophytes together to grow in deepening their grasp of the paschal mystery and in making it part of their lives through meditation on the Gospel, sharing in the eucharist, and doing the works of charity. To strengthen the neophytes as they begin to walk in newness of life, the community of the faithful, their godparents, and their parish priests (pastors) should give them thoughtful and friendly help . . . Just as their new participation in the sacraments enlightens the neophytes' understanding of the Scriptures, so too it increases their contact with the rest of the faithful and has an impact on the experience of the community. As a result, interaction between the neophytes and the faithful is made easier and more beneficial. The period of postbaptismal catechesis is of great significance for both the neophytes and the rest of the faithful. Through it the neophytes, with the help of their godparents, should experience a full and joyful welcome into the community and enter into closer ties with the other faithful. The faithful, in turn, should derive from it a renewal of inspiration and of outlook.[10]

The aim of the period of post-baptismal catechesis is clear: for neophytes to deepen their experience of faith, for them to grow spiritually, and for them to enter more into the life of the Christian community. Of course, this has implications for the members of that community, too: the RCIA is not a one-way process.

REFLECTION

- Is handing on faith just completing a course or a programme, or is it a process?
- Would Catholics who perhaps no longer practise their faith

benefit from the RCIA? Is the RCIA really just a posh 'refresher course', a 'top-up' for those who might have been absent for a while?

- What is your experience of neophytes? What witness have you shown them, what will they have learned from you?
- Think of the last time someone was received into the Catholic Church in your parish. What benefits did *you* gain? What did you offer? Did it renew your own faith in any way?
- What is the role of committed Catholics in the RCIA?

How is the RCIA celebrated in the parish?

The word 'Rite' in the title *Rite of Christian Initiation of Adults* points to the fact that this way of receiving new members into the community of the faithful is marked by public rituals, 'rites', which provide a sharp contrast to the private instruction of other eras. It is yet another aspect of the role of the community in the RCIA and is a return to the practice in the early Church where distinct periods in the initiation process were marked by rites.

The RCIA, as we have seen, depends upon candidates taking a number of decisions in the course of their journey in faith. In a sense, it is these decisions which are publicly celebrated in the parish community. The first step to be celebrated in ritual is that from inquirer to catechumen. The Rite of Acceptance marks that entrance into the catechumenate:

> Assembling publicly for the first time, the candidates who have completed the period of the precatechumenate declare their intention to the Church and the Church in turn, carrying out its apostolic mission, accepts them as persons who intend to become its members . . . The prerequisite for making this first step is that the beginnings of the spiritual life and the fundamentals of Christian teaching have taken root in the candidates.[11]

The RCIA declares that the catechumens 'are now part of the household of Christ'.[12]

The catechumenate ends with the Rite of Election on the first

Sunday of Lent. Again, a public ritual celebrates God's choice, or election, of those catechumens who are now moving towards reception into the Church at Easter. Another name for this rite is the Rite of Enrolment of Names, since 'as a pledge of fidelity the candidates inscribe their names in the book that lists those who have been chosen for initiation'.[13] This practice dates from the early centuries of Christian initiation, when candidates inscribed their names in the Book of Life. 'In the early Church, this baptismal registry was carefully guarded during times of persecution – in the wrong hands, it served as a virtual death warrant for those whose names appeared in its pages'.[14] Knowing this to be the case, how courageous it was for people to write their names in the Book of Life. This, too, might provoke us into reflecting on what is the real significance of our names in the baptismal register.

During the Lenten retreat-like Period of Purification and Enlightenment, the public rites to be celebrated are called 'Scrutinies', rites for self-searching and repentance:

> The scrutinies are meant to uncover, then heal all that is weak, defective, or sinful in the hearts of the elect; to bring out, then strengthen all that is upright, strong and good. For the scrutinies are celebrated in order to deliver the elect from the power of sin and Satan, to protect them against temptation, and to give them strength in Christ, who is the way, the truth, and the life. These rites, therefore, should complete the conversion of the elect and deepen their resolve to hold fast to Christ and to carry out their decision to love God above all.[15]

The Scrutinies, usually celebrated on the Third, Fourth and Fifth Sundays of Lent, do not entail some sort of examination of the elect. But they do include an exorcism, so that the elect, 'who have already learned from the Church as their mother the mystery of deliverance from sin by Christ, are freed from the effects of sin and from the influence of the devil. They receive new strength in the midst of their spiritual journey and they open their hearts to receive the gifts of the Saviour'.[16] The word 'exorcism' might conjure up images of evil spirits screaming or hissing as they are cast out. Exorcism in the RCIA is a far cry from this. It suggests prayers that the crushing yoke of Satan may be exchanged for the gentle yoke of Jesus. It is not for casting out devils but is a liberating experience, part of the journey to wholeness which is union with Jesus Christ.

Equally powerful rites are the Presentation of the Creed and the Lord's Prayer. These rites, celebrated during the period of Purification and Enlightenment, hark back directly to the time of the early Church. These are the basic texts that were – and still are – the foundation of the faith expressed by Christians. These are highly symbolic moments, which the RCIA says, should happen at a weekday celebration after the Scrutinies. The Latin phrase *traditio symboli* implies the handing on, or over, of the symbols and statements of faith, the Creed and Lord's Prayer. Again, in a direct return to the practice of the early Church, the elect are encouraged to memorise these texts, so that at the Easter Vigil, celebrating the sacraments of initiation, they can hand them back – *redditio symboli* – to the community.

Catechesis and the Rite of Christian Initiation of Adults

The catechetical principles behind the RCIA gave a fresh impetus to the whole understanding of handing on faith. One-to-one instruction, based perhaps largely on information about faith, was replaced by a vision which is about growing *into* and *in* faith. Catechesis is more than just instruction. The rites suggest that faith is something to be celebrated in and with the community, which itself has an important role to play. In the RCIA, the links between catechesis and liturgy are insepar-able. The faith handed on is celebrated in the Church's liturgy, and the Church's liturgy feeds back into the catechesis which can help explain the nature of celebration and worship. The journey of faith is not just catechetical, it is also liturgical. Faith is not intellectual assent, it is something which must be expressed in praise of God, in the worship of the community gathered together. The complex role of the catechist is summed up thus in the Introduction to the *Rite*: 'When they are teaching, catechists should see that their instruction is filled with the spirit of the Gospel, adapted to the liturgical signs and the cycle of the Church's year, suited to the needs of the catechumens, and as far as possible enriched by local traditions'.[17] This last phrase reveals the importance of inculturation. Handing on the faith must be rooted in the culture of the candidates so that the message of the gospel resonates in their world.

What of the catechist? The catechist is not simply handing on knowledge, but, by word and example, is helping the candidates to grow in and towards faith. It is the catechist, first of all, who must be a person of prayer, filled with the spirit of the gospel, active in a life of service in the community. It is the catechist who is one of the first examples of faith for the candidates.

It is important, too, for catechists to have some grasp of how adults learn. A catechist is not someone with all the answers. A good catechist appreciates that he or she, too, is on a journey of faith and is learning with the candidates. 'Taking people where they are' is a well-worn phrase, but an essential one in trying to understand how adults learn. Their motivation will be varied, from those perhaps just wanting to be with a group to those definitely seeking something. One of the first things to remember is that the physical environment where the learning is to take place must be welcoming. Adults must feel welcomed and comfortable. Cold parish halls on a damp, winter evening are not good for any process of handing on faith! In working with adults, it is important to acknowledge that they learn at their own pace, and are independent learners. This is an important principle in the RCIA, where decisions to take the next step in the journey of faith must be taken by the candidate. What adults may be seeking from the catechist is guidance.

Adults tend to be very practical in their learning and are keen to know what relevance the learning has in daily life. What difference will it make? How does it change my life? What relevance does the gospel message have today? In handing on faith, it is particularly important to address these issues.

Adults come to learning with a vast array of experiences, attitudes and stories. Learning must take account of these experiences and so the teaching process of adult education must both draw out and impart. Learning must build on those experiences and be careful not to reject them as insignificant. It may be stating the obvious but it is important that adults are recognised and valued as adults. It would be wrong to communicate in any way that a particular individual, coming with a unique story and set of experiences, is in some way inferior.

Although much has been written, and could still be written, about how adults learn and how the best results can be achieved, it is important for the catechist to keep in mind six basic principles: adults learn best when they feel secure and comfortable; adults learn best when they are aware of where the process is going and what the objectives are; adults learn best when their needs are being met; adults learn best when they are actively involved; adults learn best when what is being taught is relevant to their experience; adults learn best when they can see they are achieving something, they are progressing on their own journey.

A number of these points about adult learning and the role of the catechist were made in a 1990 document, *Adult Catechesis in the Christian Community – Some Principles and Guidelines*. This was published by the International Council for Catechesis following their plenary session in Rome in October 1988 dedicated to the theme 'Catechesis of Adults in the Christian Community'. In just over thirty pages this document makes many statements which are a strong challenge to any Christian community today, even declaring that it is 'not only legitimate, but necessary, to acknowledge that a fully Christian community can exist only when a systematic catechesis of all its members takes place and when an effective and well-developed catechesis of adults is regarded as the *central task* in the catechetical enterprise'.[18]

Some very practical points are made by this document, calling for a more adequate language of faith which will be comprehensible to adults at all levels, for more accessible places where un-churched adults will feel welcomed, and 'a more visible expression of sensitivity, availability and openness on the part of clergy and Church institutions towards adults, their problems and their need for catechesis'.[19] Adult catechesis is about formation, not just information, and it is rightly noted that adults 'do not grow in faith primarily by learning concepts, but by sharing the life of the Christian community, of which adults are members who both give and receive from the community'.[20]

Adult Catechesis in the Christian Community goes on to talk about the practical implementations of the vision of catechesis it offers. The goal of adult catechesis is clear: to help the mature Christian to live as an adult in the world by acquiring certain qualities. But this is just a starting-point for those who are catechised, for 'catechesis must help adults to learn not only for themselves, but should prepare them to *communicate the contents of faith to others* . . . showing other adults what an impact the faith can have on their lives and on the world around them'.[21] An important point for all Christians to remember is that ongoing catechesis calls us to be evangelisers.

From an important methodological view, the document recognises the questions that adults might have and states that these cannot be overlooked:

> In the presentation of the Christian religion, catechesis must deal with the many *questions*, difficulties and doubts which arise in the human heart. Indeed, these questions should be brought to light when they have been obscured or confused by ignorance or indifference. The faith response to these questions will appear meaningful if it is rooted in the Bible and in concrete historical life, and if it is respectful of reason and attentive to the signs of the times.[22]

The tension raised by this point is important to bear in mind. Some people would argue that catechesis is simply about handing on Truth, a Truth that can never be questioned and must be adhered to at all times. *Adult Catechesis in the Christian Community* acknowledges that questions will arise and must not be ignored. Catechesis is a two-way dialogue between catechist and recipient, not a one-way lecture:

> Of fundamental importance is the *dialogical approach* which, while recognizing that all are called to the obedience of faith, respects the basic freedom and autonomy of adults and encourages them to engage in an open and cordial dialogue . . . Moreover, the truths of faith should be pre-

sented as certitudes, without taking away from the fact that for pilgrims on their way towards the full revelation of truth and life, the path of research and investigation always remains open.[23]

There is a tension acknowledged here which catechesis must try to balance to be faithful to its task.

The ministry of the catechist does not mean the catechist is superior to those being catechised. The catechist, too, is part of the journey of faith:

> Stability and living the Christian faith as a member of the ecclesial community are basic requirements for catechists. They must mature as spiritual persons in the concrete tasks they perform, in such a way that the 'first word' they speak is that of personal witness ... an indispensable quality of catechists is the wise insight which allows them to go beyond the interpretation of texts to a deep grasp of vital issues and contemporary problems, and to be able to critically interpret present day events and the 'signs of the times'.[24]

At the heart of catechesis is the inculturation of the faith.

REFLECTION

- The RCIA is the definitive model of catechesis, offering a norm for all catechesis. 'It is both model and norm because it takes the people where they are, as seekers, inquirers, candidates, catechumens or neophytes and leads them, with the local community through the liturgical rites, to embrace the paschal mystery as their own mystery'.[25] Any comment?
- 'The specific role of the catechesis of adults consists in an initial deepening of the faith received at baptism, in an elementary, complete and systematic way, with a view to helping individuals all life long grow to the full maturity of Christ'.[26] Comments? Is this definition helpful in setting goals?
- *Adult Catechesis in the Christian Community* refers to the parish as the 'privileged place' of catechesis. It is there that 'cat-

echesis is realized not only through formal instruction, but also in the liturgy, sacraments and charitable activity'.[27] How do you perceive catechesis in these different activities?

- *Adult Catechesis in the Christian Community* lists some of the characteristics of the catechist as the ability to listen and dialogue, encourage and reassure, form relationships, work in teams, and build community. 'In a word, the catechist of adults will be a sufficiently balanced human being, with the flexibility to adapt to different circumstances'.[28] How would you envisage some of these qualities being used? Why do you think they are important?

5 *A New* Catechism *and a New* Directory

On 29 May 1994 the English translation of the *Catechism of the Catholic Church* was published. It was the first Catechism for the universal Church to be published for more than four hundred years (the *Roman Catechism* of the Council of Trent had been published in 1566). Worldwide reaction was varied. 'Catholics are split on new Catechism,' proclaimed one newspaper. 'Rome's new catechism is anti-capitalist, up-to-date and utterly traditional,' said another. A catechism, as already seen in the catechisms of earlier centuries, is a text summarising fundamental truths which the Church believes. It is the sort of document intended to help Church members and others to understand their faith. The response to the *Catechism* was immediate, and, if its impact were to be measured in terms of sales, it is an unprecedented success. In France, where the *Catechism* was first published in 1992, it became an overnight bestseller, eagerly snapped up even at airport bookshops! In England, 100,000 copies were sold within a fortnight of publication, and in the United States half a million copies had been ordered *before* publication.

But sales do not really measure the true impact of a book. The publication of the new *Catechism* raised the fundamental question as to just how such a traditional text fits in with the documents that had immediately preceded it, such as the *General Catechetical Directory* (1971) and *Adult Catechesis in the Christian Community* (1990)? Again, opinions vary. 'On the one hand are those who see in [the *Catechism*] a safeguard for the Church's unity of faith in the context of an emerging planetary culture. On the other hand are those who see in it the dead hand of centralised uniformity hostile to the necessity of earthing catechetics in local cultures'.[1] Indeed, one commentator said that 'the local churches no more need this kind of catechism than the African Synod needs the Vatican as a meeting place'.[2]

Where did the Catechism of the Catholic Church come from?

The First Vatican Council (1869–70) had, as I have already outlined, proposed a universal catechism for children. Such a text was never produced, and although a similar proposal was discussed at the Second Vatican Council, a universal catechism was still not forthcoming. But the desire for such a text never went away. As the bishops gathered for the first Synod of Bishops in 1967, the idea of a universal catechism arose once again. Controversy had been sparked by the publication of the Dutch Catechism in 1966. Now some bishops were beginning to ask for a clarificatory catechism to act as a rule of faith. Pope Paul VI still favoured a General Directory, and partly in response to the bishops' request he published his *Creed of the People of God* in 1968 (this text is now popularly referred to simply as Pope Paul VI's *Credo*). Despite the 1971 publication of the *General Catechetical Directory* some bishops still saw the need for a catechism, and the tension between the uniformity of doctrinal expression they desired and the need for inculturation surfaced in some of the interventions at both the 1974 Synod of Bishops on evangelisation and the 1977 Synod on catechesis. The bishops were still undecided. Some wanted a short catechism for children, others wanted a catechism of the teachings of the Second Vatican Council, and still others wanted a universal catechism.

The document that came out of the 1977 Synod, *Catechesis in our Time*, was prepared by Pope John Paul II. He referred to the *General Catechetical Directory* as the 'standard of reference' and then wrote:

> In this regard, I must warmly encourage the Episcopal Conferences of the whole world to undertake, patiently but resolutely, the considerable work to be accomplished in agreement with the Apostolic See in order to prepare genuine catechisms which will be faithful to the essential

content of revelation and up to date in method, and which will be capable of educating the Christian generations of the future to a sturdy faith.[3]

Just under twenty years later, at another gathering of bishops for the Extraordinary Synod of 1985 to commemorate the twentieth anniversary of the Second Vatican Council, a resolution for a universal catechism was put forward. By now the catechetical climate was somewhat different. In the early 1980s there was growing unease among some of the bishops at the direction religious education and catechesis were taking. Some texts were seen as suspect, most notably the French bishops' text for children, *Pierres Vivantes,* and the American text *Christ Among Us.*[4] There was still a tension between the emphases on content and process, with many texts emphasising the theory in handing on faith as envisaged by the Second Vatican Council. Such texts point to the vision of catechesis as a lifelong activity aimed at fostering and maturing faith celebrated in liturgy. But there was also the need to be clear about the content of that faith, as expressed by the Church down the centuries.

Catechisms that state the content of faith need plenty of expertise and resources. At the Extraordinary Synod in 1985, the bishops of Korea, Senegal and Mauritius, countries with limited catechetical resources, first expressed the need for a universal catechism. Their request was formally put forward by Cardinal Bernard Law of Boston, who asked that 'a catechism or compendium of all Catholic doctrine regarding both faith and morals be composed, that it might be, as it were, a point of reference for the catechisms or compendiums that are prepared in the various countries.'[5]

And so the journey towards the *Catechism* had begun. Significantly, the *Catechism* was to be a reference-point for local catechisms, implying that it was a text more to do with unity of faith than uniformity. Adaptation was key and this, too, suggests that it was to be a text in line with the *General Catechetical Directory.* It was not a 'Vatican document' but was the result of worldwide consultation (more than 24,000 amendments were received to draft texts sent out). Whereas previous catechisms very much provided the content of faith for all believers, the

Catechism of the Catholic Church had a specific audience in mind. It was addressed first of all to the bishops, the primary teachers of the faith, and then to compilers of catechisms, and through them to the people of God. First and foremost, the *Catechism* was meant to be a resource for teachers of catechesis to help in compiling local catechisms.

This context for the *Catechism* is important. What was published, first in French in 1992 and then in English in 1994, was not a 'Vatican' document, nor an answer to contemporary debates, nor a 'how-to-do-it-properly' book, nor a stick with which to beat people. The *Catechism of the Catholic Church* is an important catechetical document. It is a world document and so it cannot take into account every aspect of all the cultures in which the gospel is to be proclaimed. It cannot, therefore, and does not attempt to impose a method of catechesis. It is a text which bishops and their collaborators in catechesis are invited to reflect on so that their catechetical initiatives may be enriched. The *Catechism* itself must be inculturated.

REFLECTION

- In 1993, Cardinal Sanchez, then Prefect of the Congregation for the Clergy, said that the sheer size and depth of the *Catechism* meant that it should not be used as a basic textbook for catechists. Nor should the 'In Brief' summaries at the end of each section be used as a basic text. He believed that the *Catechism* presented 'the unique and essential content' which is Catholic doctrine, 'while leaving to catechists and their catechetical material (not catechisms) the task of inculturating and incarnating the message'. How does this balance between catechism and catechesis strike you? How can it be practically applied?
- Why is the *Catechism* a point of reference?
- Can a world document like the *Catechism* really be 'inculturated'? How can the request of the bishops of Korea, Senegal and Mauritius have echoes in each local church? How can a 700-page book answer their needs?

Catechesis and the Catechism of the Catholic Church

In April 1994 the Catholic Bishops of England and Wales published some *Guidelines for the Use of the Catechism of the Catholic
Church*. They noted that the *Catechism* had been published to
carry forward the work of the Second Vatican Council and
located the text firmly within a new initiative in evangelisation
and catechesis:

> The work of catechesis can never stand still . . . Those res-
> ponsible for catechesis and religious education face a dual
> task; they must faithfully reflect on the whole range and
> richness of faith and belief which we desire to share;
> and, through the creative adaptation of methods and
> materials, they must try to communicate that rich vision
> of faith to today's seekers. The Catechism meets the
> requirements of the first task . . . [6]

Communicating the faith to today's seekers represents an
enormous challenge, for it means that inculturation must be at
the heart of the task in hand. A credible account of faith is
needed. To a certain extent, this is what the *Catechism* attempts
to offer: 'The Catechism emphasizes the exposition of doctrine.
It seeks to help deepen understanding of faith. In this way it is
oriented towards the maturing of that faith, its putting down
roots in personal life, and its shining forth in personal conduct'.[7]
This is the 'what' of faith. The 'how', the catechetical methodology, is the responsibility of those who instruct the faithful.
On this matter the *Catechism* of 1994 at this point quotes the
Roman Catechism of 1566: 'Those who are called to the ministry
of preaching must suit their words to the maturity and understanding of their hearers, as they hand on the teaching of the
mysteries of faith and the rules of moral conduct'.[8]

This point is central to the work of catechesis envisaged by
the *Catechism*. In listing the adaptations that will be necessary
the *Catechism* speaks of adaptation according to differences of
culture, age, spiritual life, and social and ecclesial conditions
of the faithful, of the need to use different teaching methods,
and of the need to present the faith according to the maturity
and understanding of the hearers. It is a clear call to root the

message of the gospel in the culture of today, and to link it
with the human experiences of the faithful.

Without this creative interaction with human experience
and contemporary culture, there is the danger that we may
end up passing on the dead faith of the living instead of
the living faith of the dead. In this regard it is important
to remember what John Paul II said about the process of
inculturation: 'A faith which does not become culture is a
faith which has not been fully received, nor thoroughly
thought through, nor fully lived out'.[9]

Much of what the *Catechism* has to say specifically about
catechesis is taken from the 1979 document, *Catechesis in our
Time*. Catechesis is about putting people in communion with
Jesus Christ: 'It is by looking to him in faith that Christ's faithful
can hope that he himself fulfils his promises in them, and that,
by loving him with the same love with which he has loved
them, they may perform works in keeping with their dignity'.[10]
The *Catechism* also speaks of the inseparable link between
catechesis and the liturgy, the privileged place for catechising.
The comment on liturgy and catechesis offers an interesting
insight into catechetical methodology: 'Liturgical catechesis
aims to initiate people into the mystery of Christ (it is
"mystagogy") by proceeding from the visible to the invisible,
from the sign to the thing signified. Such catechesis is to be
presented by local and regional catechisms'.[11] 'From the visible
to the invisible' could be seen as an endorsement of the importance of experience in catechesis. A particular method in
catechesis can begin with experience and shed the light of
Christ upon it, proceeding from the sign to the thing signified.
The structure of the *Catechism* itself says something about
catechesis. It is divided into four parts: The Profession of Faith,
Celebration of Faith, Life in Christ, and Christian Prayer. Just
as in the early Church handing on faith began with the Creed,
so the *Catechism* at the end of the second millennium begins
with the Creed, the original baptismal catechesis. The significance is evident: 'The linking of the doctrine of the faith to the
baptismal profession of faith also makes it clear that catechesis
is not simply the communication of a religious theory. Rather,

it intends to set a life-process in motion: namely, growth in the life given through baptism, growth in communion with God'.[12] Faith is not a finished business that can be ticked off as completed. Catechesis is not mere instruction, but adaptation to God's ways.

REFLECTION

- 'With the publication of the *Catechism of the Catholic Church,* we have an authoritative, reliable *regula fidei*; but the Catechism leaves to catechists the task of making the faith come alive in the hearts and minds of individuals'.[13] What do you remember about the *Catechism* and its publication in 1994? How have you experienced it being used? How do you think it should be used by catechists?
- What sort of book do you think the *Catechism* is?
- Given the developments in catechesis since the Second Vatican Council do you think the *Catechism* has a role to play? Is it the right sort of book at the right time?

General Directory for Catechesis

In October 1997 an International Catechetical Congress took place in Rome on the theme 'The Faith of the Church and Its Evangelizing Mission'. It was more than twenty-five years since the publication of the *General Catechetical Directory* and the Congress introduced a revised text of that document, the *General Directory for Catechesis.* The Congress was organised by the Congregation for the Clergy, the Vatican department responsible for catechesis, and was attended by more than two hundred bishops, priests, religious and lay people from seventy-three different countries. They reflected on and discussed the reception and use of the *Catechism of the Catholic Church* and the new *Directory* now before them.

The revision of the 1971 *Directory* was prompted by the publication of the *Catechism*. Just as the 1971 text reflected the catechetical vision of the Second Vatican Council, so the new *General Directory for Catechesis* takes on the vision of the *Cat-*

echism. If the *Catechism* is the 'what' of handing on faith, then the *Directory* is the 'how', offering guidance and encouragement for the indispensable adaptation the *Catechism* requires. The *Catechism* emphasised doctrine and not methodology; now, the *General Directory for Catechesis* provides

> the basic principles of pastoral theology taken from the Magisterium of the Church, and in a special way from the Second Vatican Council by which pastoral action in the ministry of the word can be more fittingly directed and governed ... [It is] an official aid for the transmission of the Gospel message and for the whole of catechetical activity ... [and] simply seeks to facilitate a better understanding and use of the *Catechism of the Catholic Church* in catechetical practice.[14]

The new *Directory* takes into account some of the problems encountered in catechesis over the years since the Second Vatican Council. These included a declining reference to the role of Tradition and almost exclusive use of Scripture alone, and an over-emphasis on just the humanity of the person of Jesus Christ, or, in some cases, just the divinity, so that a more balanced presentation is needed. The *Directory* also noted certain

> doctrinal *lacunae* concerning the truth about God and man; about sin and grace and about eschatology; there is a need for a more solid moral formation; presentations of the history of the Church are inadequate; and too little importance is given to her social teaching; in some regions there has been a proliferation of catechisms and texts, the products of particular initiatives whose selective tendencies and emphases are so differing as to damage that convergence necessary for the unity of the faith.[15]

It also warned of a possible weak link between catechesis and liturgy and the temptation 'to fall into a "content-method" dualism, with resultant reductionism to one or other extreme'.[16]

This last point is important, for the field of catechetics has always been struggling with the tension of the content–method dualism, a catechesis led by doctrinal propositions or a catechesis with a person-centred approach. There are those who believe handing on faith must be content-led and there are those who believe it is the process which is all-important, beginning with people's experience. The 1997 International Catechetical Congress and the *General Directory for Catechesis* seemed to acknowledge the virtual impossibility of separating content from method. Catechesis is not just about content, but nor is it just about method.

What the *Directory* says about methodology is important:

> The principle of 'fidelity to God and fidelity to man' leads to an avoidance of any opposition or artificial separation or presumed neutrality between method and content. It affirms, rather, their necessary correlation and interaction. The catechist recognizes that method is at the service of revelation and conversion, and that therefore it is necessary to make use of it. The catechist knows that the content of catechesis cannot be indifferently subjected to any method. It requires a process of transmission which is adequate to the nature of the message, to its sources and language, to the concrete circumstances of ecclesial communities as well as to the particular circumstances of the faithful to whom catechesis is addressed ... A good catechetical method is a guarantee of fidelity to content.[17]

How, then, are we to understand catechesis? The *Directory* is straightforward and for its definition returns to the 1979 document *Catechesis in our Time*: 'The definitive aim of catechesis is to put people not only in touch, but also in communion and intimacy, with Jesus Christ'.[18] And the *Directory* goes on: 'It proposes to help those who have just converted "to know better this Jesus to whom he has entrusted himself: to know his 'mystery', the kingdom of God proclaimed by him, the requirements and comments contained in his Gospel message, and the paths that he has laid down for anyone who wishes to follow him" '.[19]

Catechesis is rooted in the person of Jesus Christ, but this education in and to faith is not something passive. It includes

more than instruction: it is an apprenticeship of the entire

Christian life ... which promotes an authentic following
of Christ, focused on his Person; it implies education in
knowledge of the faith and in the life of faith, in such a
manner that the entire person ... feels enriched by the
word of God; it helps the disciple of Christ to transform
the old man in order to assume his baptismal responsibilities and to profess the faith from the heart.[20]

The tasks of catechesis are listed as promoting knowledge of
the faith, liturgical education, moral formation, and teaching to
pray. This is not done in any isolation, for catechesis must
prepare the Christian to live in community and to participate
actively in the life and mission of the Church.

The *Directory* notes that there are two principal means for
carrying out the tasks of catechesis: transmission of the gospel
message and experience of the Christian life. 'Every dimension
of the faith, like the faith itself as a whole, must be rooted in
human experience and not remain a mere adjunct to the human
person. Knowledge of the faith is significant. It gives light to the
whole of existence and dialogues with culture'.[21] This complex
relationship between the Christian message and human experience is not just a question of getting the right methodological
balance. Experience has different functions in catechesis which
must be carefully evaluated. Catechesis must make people
aware of their own experiences so that, in the light of the gospel,
they can judge the questions and needs that spring from them.
Experience is also a way of exploring and assimilating the
truths of faith.

Interpreting and illuminating experience with the data of
faith is a constant task of catechetical pedagogy – even if
with difficulty. It is a task that cannot be overlooked
without falling into artificial juxtapositions or closed
understandings of the truth. It is made possible, however,
by a correct application of the correlation and interaction
between profound human experiences and the revealed
message.[22]

In catechesis, there is not one single method which is to be
preferred above all others. Variety of methods is in fact a sign

of life and is required by the age and intellectual development of those to be catechised, their degree of ecclesial and spiritual maturity and many other circumstances. Two methods of note are the inductive and deductive methods. These are also called 'kerygmatic' and 'existential'. The former begins with the proclamation of the message expressed in the principal documents of the faith and applies it to life, while the latter moves from human problems and conditions and enlightens them with the Word of God. A still valid catechetical method is that of memorization of texts, particularly the principal formulae of the faith. However, the *Directory* warns against any mere 'mechanical memorization' and states clearly that any texts committed to memory should, of course, be explained first.

Like earlier Church documents, the *General Directory for Catechesis* reaffirms the primary role of catechesis for adults. This is the chief form of catechesis to which all other forms should in some way be oriented. 'This implies that the catechesis of other age groups should have it for a point of reference and should be expressed in conjunction with it, in a coherent catechetical programme suitable to meet the pastoral needs of dioceses'.[23] Although it cannot be within the scope of this work to examine the *Directory* section by section, it is worth noting that a substantial part of the document is devoted to the particular needs and concerns of those to be catechised. Part Four of the *Directory* is divided into sections looking at catechesis according to age, catechesis for special situations, mentalities and environments, catechesis in the socio-religious context, and catechesis in the socio-cultural context.

The *General Directory for Catechesis* sees catechesis as inextricably linked with evangelisation, an essential moment in the process of evangelisation. In Part One of the *Directory,* entitled 'Catechesis in the Church's mission of evangelization', it is stated that catechesis

> transmits the words and deeds of Revelation; it is obliged to proclaim and narrate them and, at the same time, to make clear the profound mysteries they contain. Moreover, since Revelation is a source of light for the human person,

catechesis not only recalls the marvels worked by God in
the past, but also, in the light of the same Revelation, it
interprets the signs of the times and the present life of man,
since it is in these that the plan of God for the salvation of
the world is realized.[24]

Once again, the importance of inculturation, rooting the
gospel message in the culture of the time, is clear. It can be said
that one of the chief thrusts of the *Directory* is in fact inculturation, the pattern for which is the 'original inculturation', the
incarnation, the Word made flesh. The document calls for
the 'drawing up of local catechisms which respond to the
demands of different cultures and which present the Gospel in
relation to the hopes, questions and problems which these cultures present'.[25] Furthermore, the catechumenate and
catechetical institutes are called 'centres of inculturation' which
incorporate the language, symbols and values of the cultures
in which they are rooted. But great care must be taken in
incarnating the gospel in society: 'It is not simply an external
adaptation designed to make the Christian message more attrac-
tive or superficially decorative. On the contrary, it means the
penetration of the deepest strata of persons and peoples by
the Gospel which touches them deeply, "going to the very
centre and roots" of their cultures'.[26]

REFLECTION

- 'The [1997] congress considered the Catechism and the Directory as a whole. The one without the other is no more
  catechesis than a white or a yolk alone is an egg'.[27] How do
  you perceive the relationship between the *Catechism of the
  Catholic Church* and the *General Directory for Catechesis?* Why
  do you think one received lots of publicity when published
  while the other did not? Does this say something about a
  general perception of what is important in handing on faith?
- 'The aim of catechetical activity consists in precisely this: to
  encourage a living, explicit and fruitful profession of faith.
  The Church, in order to achieve this, transmits to catechumens and those to be catechized, her living experience

of the Gospel, her faith, so that they may appropriate and profess it. Hence, "authentic catechesis is always an orderly and systematic initiation into the revelation that God has given of himself to humanity in Christ Jesus, a revelation stored in the depths of the Church's memory and in Sacred Scripture, and constantly communicated from one generation to the next by a living active *traditio*" '.[28] How helpful is this? What do the following phrases mean to you: 'a living, explicit and fruitful profession of faith', 'living experience of the Gospel', and 'a living active *traditio* [tradition]'?

- The *General Directory for Catechesis* said much about the need for inculturation. How do you think this is reflected in religious language? Is religious language still meaningful today?

- The *Directory* states that the media and all means of social communication are essential for evangelisation and catechesis (nn. 160ff.). How do you understand this? How can modern information technology contribute to the work of catechesis?

- 'No methodology, no matter how well tested, can dispense with the person of the catechist in every phase of the catechetical process. The charism given . . . by the Spirit, a solid spirituality and transparent witness of life, constitutes the soul of every method'.[29] What hopes and fears does this raise? What do you think makes a person the best teacher of faith?

Part Two –

Catechesis: Into the Parish

The history of catechesis shows how various attempts have been made to hand on faith in varying circumstances. Manuals, catechisms, directories, word-of-mouth, example, have all played their part. Key words or even opposites reveal the shifting emphases: conversion and knowledge, heart faith and head faith, growth in community and growth in private, journey and arrival, faith and 'The Faith', formation and information, mystery and fact, values and laws. All have their role to play.

Catechesis is not just history or theory. The challenge is now to take into the parish community a vision and ministry of catechesis built on the good practice seen over the centuries. It is a catechesis rooted in Scripture, Tradition, and Church teaching, and nourished by prayer.

> In positive terms, a catechesis which inspires not only intellectual assimilation of the faith, but also touches the heart and transforms conduct is correct. Catechesis, thus, generates a dynamic life which is unified by the faith. It bridges the gap between belief and life, between the Christian message and the cultural context, and brings forth the fruits of true holiness. (*General Directory for Catechesis*, n. 205)

This is the challenge for the parish community in its ministry of handing on faith.

6 So What About Catechesis Today?

In 1992, with the publication of the first edition of the *Catechism of the Catholic Church*, Pope John Paul II asked that this text be used 'assiduously in fulfilling [the] mission of proclaiming the faith and calling people to the Gospel life ... The *Catechism of the Catholic Church* ... is offered to every individual who asks us to give an account of the hope that is in us (cf. *1 Peter 3:15*) and who wants to know what the Catholic Church believes'.[1] More than 1500 years earlier, St Augustine had written: 'And to impart such instruction, it will not suffice to place a small manual in one's hand; rather it will be necessary to enkindle a great zeal in one's heart'.[2] The balance between these two statements is the challenge of catechesis today.

The picture today

What picture are we faced with today? What is the backdrop against which we are trying to hand on faith? Several images of important moments in celebrating faith spring to mind. One can think of parishes where there is a wonderful celebration of the sacraments of initiation at the Easter Vigil, with a number of people welcomed into the new life of the Christian community; or parish celebrations where the bishop confirms young people who have really thought about their faith and *confirm* what they believe in the midst of the community to which they belong. But there is another side to the coin. Someone once said that every day more and more people are leaving the Church and returning to God. And there is the hopefully apocryphal story of a mother who took a photograph of the very moment of her child's First Communion, as the priest offered her daughter the Body of Christ. 'Father,' mum said almost immediately, 'could you give her another one because the flash on the camera didn't work!'; and one can't forget couples who go to their parish priest to ask how much it will cost to get married, with the implication that price is the determining factor.

It is against such a varied backdrop – of good, bad and indifferent experiences – that catechesis takes place today. But how is catechesis to respond to such a variety of situations?

There are many models of catechesis, many approaches which offer a way of responding to the situation presented to us by Church and society. I believe one of the best models is that offered by the American Maronite priest Fr Dominic Ashkar. Having worked for many years as a Director of Religious Education in Washington, DC, Dominic Ashkar has wide experience of handing on faith with various groups. His vision of catechesis saw that clearly this was not just handing on a certain amount of information but was a life-long journey rooted in a community. Even more, it was a journey made *with* that community, not outside it, with a view to joining at a later date. Catechesis is about journeying with, not arriving at.

Fr Ashkar's vision of catechesis is contained in his book *Road to Emmaus – A New Model for Catechesis*, published in 1993. As the title suggests, Ashkar bases catechesis on the Emmaus story from Luke's Gospel. This shows that catechesis is not just a modern, posh invention by the Church but is part of the missionary task entrusted to it and rooted in the mission of Jesus himself, the supreme Teacher and Catechist.

> The encounter on the road to Emmaus was not learning *about* Jesus Christ, nor was it abstract theology. Emmaus was not a course in religion as something to *appreciate*, or something to *have* or *believe*. Emmaus was an encounter. It began with Jesus' approach to discouraged disciples, and it continued in several stages of his questioning, listening, and explanation – based on their needs.[3]

A reminder of Luke's story:

> That very same day, two of them were on their way to a village called Emmaus, seven miles from Jerusalem, and

they were talking together about all that had happened. Now as they talked this over, Jesus himself came up and walked by their side; but something prevented them from recognising him. He said to them, 'What matters are you discussing as you walk along?' They stopped short, their faces downcast.

Then one of them, called Cleopas, answered him, 'You must be the only person staying in Jerusalem who does not know the things that have been happening there these last few days'. 'What things?' he asked. 'All about Jesus of Nazareth' they answered 'who proved he was a great prophet by the things he said and did in the sight of God and of the whole people; and how our chief priests and our leaders handed him over to be sentenced to death, and had him crucified. Our own hope had been that he would be the one to set Israel free. And this is not all: two whole days have gone by since it all happened; and some women from our group have astounded us: they went to the tomb in the early morning, and when they did not find the body, they came back to tell us they had seen a vision of angels who declared he was alive. Some of our friends went to the tomb and found everything exactly as the women had reported, but of him they saw nothing.'

Then he said to them, 'You foolish men! So slow to believe the full message of the prophets! Was it not ordained that the Christ should suffer and so enter into his glory?' Then, starting with Moses and going through all the prophets, he explained to them the passages throughout the scriptures that were about himself.

When they drew near to the village to which they were going, he made as if to go on; but they pressed him to stay with them. 'It is nearly evening' they said 'and the day is almost over.' So he went in to stay with them. Now while he was with them at table, he took the bread and said the blessing; then he broke it and handed it to them. And their eyes were opened and they recognised him; but he had vanished from their sight. Then they said to each other, 'Did not our hearts burn within us as he talked to us on the road and explained the scriptures to us?'

They set out that instant and returned to Jerusalem. There they found the Eleven assembled together with their companions, who said to them, 'Yes, it is true. The Lord has risen and has appeared to Simon.' Then they told their story of what had happened on the road and how they recognised him at the breaking of bread. (Luke 24:13–35)

The Emmaus story is perhaps one of the most memorable of the post-resurrection appearances of Jesus. Although it is not the task of this book to examine the text from the viewpoint of detailed scriptural analysis, it is noteworthy that a number of Scripture scholars refer to the unique nature of this story when compared with other accounts of Jesus' post-resurrection appearances: '(i) The two men are not leaders of the community but represent all followers of Jesus; (ii) they are troubled and do not understand why Jesus is absent; (iii) at first they do not recognize Jesus; (iv) the apostles seem to recognize Jesus but do not believe their senses; (v) after recognition, these men do not hesitate to believe; (vi) once recognized, Jesus disappears'.[4] From a catechetical point of view it is also noteworthy that Luke's story follows the pattern of the liturgy: reading and explanation of Scripture followed by the breaking of bread. Catechesis cannot be separated from the liturgy, since it both leads to it and is nourished by it.

In the Emmaus story, Dominic Ashkar finds ten catechetical principles which point to Jesus as the supreme Teacher and Catechist and provide the model for any catechist today.

Jesus the catechist/teacher	*The catechist/teacher today*
1. Jesus knew himself – what his identity was, who he was.	1. The teacher knows who he or she is.
2. Jesus knew his mission, what he was about.	2. The teacher knows his or her mission.
3. Jesus approached the disciples in person.	3. The teacher approaches the students personally.
4. Jesus walked along with them.	4. The teacher walks along with the students.
5. He said to them, 'What are you discussing as	5. The teacher finds out where the students are.

you go your way?'

6. Then he said to them, 'O foolish [dear witless] ones, slow to believe all that the prophets foretold!'	6. The teacher explains from the perspective of the students.
7. He made as if to go further.	7. The teacher invites the students to make a response.
8. Once at the table, he took bread, blessed it, broke it, and gave it to them, whereupon their eyes were opened and they recognised him.	8. The teacher leads the students to liturgy.
9. They spoke with each other.	9. The students discuss the message among themselves.
10. They got up immediately and returned to Jerusalem.	10. The students go out to share the message.

Ashkar's reflection on the Emmaus story as catechesis is a brilliant model for catechesis in a parish setting which can be applied in any situation. In his analysis the terms 'teacher' and 'student' are not, of course, strictly academic, based on a teacher–student classroom analogy. For our purposes, the term 'teacher' can be read as 'catechist', one who is working with any group of any age with a view to handing on faith. Similarly, 'student' can be anyone of any age with whom the catechist is working.

But let us look at Ashkar's ten Emmaus catechetical principles in detail.

1. Jesus knew who he was

Jesus was very clear about his relationship to his Father, the Father who had said, 'You are my Son, the Beloved; my favour rests on you' (Mark 1:11). In the whole of his life Jesus then lived out this relationship in such a way that to have seen him was to have seen the Father (cf. John 14:9). What is seen in Jesus, then, is not just abstract teaching but the very person of the Father. When it comes to the catechist, the parallel is not an obscure principle. Catechists come to their task aware of their own limitations, but, more importantly, aware of their desire to share their own faith, to share their own experiences, to share who they are. To express it in terms of the over-used jargon, they share their story of their relationship with God.

2. Jesus knew his mission

This second principle is inseparable from the first. 'The words I say to you I do not speak as from myself: it is the Father, living in me, who is doing this work ... I call you friends, because I have made known to you everything I have learnt from my Father' (John 14:10, 15:15). 'After John had been arrested, Jesus went into Galilee. There he proclaimed the Good News from God. "The time has come" he said "and the kingdom of God is close at hand. Repent, and believe the Good News" ' (Mark 1:14–15). Jesus' teaching challenged those who listened and called for a response. It was impossible to remain indifferent. He called people to a relationship with the Father and a specific way of life, so that those who responded could then themselves go out and proclaim the Good News. 'Go, therefore, make disciples of all the nations; baptise them in the name of the Father and of the Son and of the Holy Spirit, and teach them to observe all the commands I gave you. And know that I am with you always; yes, to the end of time' (Matthew 28:19–20).

There was a clear plan to Jesus' teaching. It was not just nice principles but a specific plan to bring disciples to a new way of life. Likewise, catechists today must know what they are doing. Handing on faith is not just a nice idea, a nice way of sharing stories, but is specifically aimed at proclaiming the Good News. For the catechist, this calls for careful planning in a number of areas, such as what techniques to use and how to balance content and method. The treasure of faith must not be handed on haphazardly. The catechist must be fully aware of the mission and ministry of catechesis and this implies, first of all, knowing what is the aim of any catechetical work.

3. Jesus approached the disciples in person

The initiative comes from Jesus. He seeks out the disciples on the road: 'Jesus himself came up and walked by their side' (Luke 24:15). He wants to be with the disciples, to help them at this important moment. He does not wait for them to come to him with their problems, but he goes to meet them on their journey.

The importance of this principle cannot be underestimated. Many people may have good memories of teachers at school, for example, who are remembered first of all not so much for their words but for their personal interest in pupils as human beings. Catechists must approach those they work with personally, must love them not because they are part of a group, but because they are individuals on a journey, a journey they undertake with the catechists. Being a catechist is a gesture of love not a gesture of intellect. On the road to Emmaus, the disciples recognised that Jesus approached them in person and loved them, and so their response was not to reject him but to be open with and to him. Catechists, then, must not be contrived in their approach to the people they work with, but must be open and loving. To do otherwise would run the risk of rejection of not only themselves but also the message. As Dominic Ashkar so pertinently puts it: 'From this simple, personal approach, [Jesus] set the stage for a whole catechesis. It is an example for us, as we are always tempted to think of religion as doctrine or morality, whereas Christianity is *someone*'.[5] Catechesis is rooted in a personal relationship.

4. Jesus walked along with them

The idea of journey is a popular religious theme and it has been said many times that we are all on a journey. The incarnation itself reflects this, as Jesus himself came among us at a

108   *Catechesis: Into the Parish*

specific time and place. On the road to Emmaus Jesus was not a passer-by but a fellow traveller. He did not greet the disciples and move on, but 'walked by their side' (Luke 24:15). He became their companion, a significant description in terms of this story since the word 'companion' literally means 'one who shares bread'.

Catechists, too, walk alongside their fellow travellers. They are not religious experts with all the answers, but people journeying along the same road. What unites the catechist and the one being catechised, of any age, is that they are both followers and therefore travelling companions.

5. Jesus asked the disciples a question

'What matters are you discussing as you walk along?' Jesus asked (Luke 24:17). But of course he knew the answer, for he knew everything. In one sense he could have joined them on the road and immediately calmed their fear by reassuring them that everything would be all right. Significantly, Jesus became a listener. He asked what was important to them at this particular time, and listened to their feelings about his own life and death. In today's jargon, he tries to find out where the disciples are by letting them speak about what is important to them. At this early stage of the journey he offers the disciples no doctrinal truths or content.

Jesus provides an example for catechists here as he in no way shows himself superior to the disciples. They are the starting-point, not him. Catechists must first of all be listeners, trying to understand where others are coming from rather than attempting to tell them where they will be taken. Linked with the previous principle of journeying alongside others, it is clear that the pace is not set by the catechist. Jesus walked *with* the disciples and listened to them, rather than walking ahead of them and telling them. So, although there may be a temptation to rush ahead and provide answers this must be avoided. Catechists must join others on *their* part of the journey.

6. Jesus said to them, 'O foolish ones!'

It is now that Jesus the Teacher begins to put together the pieces of the jigsaw that the disciples had not understood. As teacher he is not so much correcting their faults, but, like a friend, pointing out the direction the passages in Scripture pointed to. 'These disciples had failed to fathom any better than most of his other followers that the Messiah would be sacrificed, not honoured on a golden throne. They just "didn't get it," as we say today'.[6]

The idea of a jigsaw is useful to bear in mind in this context. Individual pieces make little sense, but the whole picture does. By looking at the completed picture on the lid of the box it is easy to see where the individual pieces fit in. The disciples were aware of these individual pieces, but didn't get the whole picture. Jesus explained it to them, just as the catechist must try to explain from the perspective of those being catechised, beginning with their experience and understanding and seeing where that fits into the whole picture.

7. Jesus made as if to go further

In many respects this is the decisive point of the journey and one of the most challenging aspects of catechesis today. Jesus has put the jigsaw together for the disciples, has explained where all the pieces fit, and thereby showed that all those passages of Scripture actually point to him. Although this calls for a response, it cannot be imposed from on high. The disciples are now called to take the next step. Jesus the Teacher has done what he can and so 'he made as if to go on' (Luke 24:28). Faith, and for the disciples on the road to Emmaus faith in the resurrection, cannot be forced upon anyone.

Dominic Ashkar's comment on this moment in the journey merits reflection:

> What a compelling model for catechists! Like Jesus, we teachers also address not just a category of people called 'students' but free persons with their own destiny, their own home in heaven. We cannot make decisions for them

once we have given them the basic information and explanation to meet their needs. We cannot choose for them, even if their choices may turn out to be unfortunate ones. To create pressure or take advantage of our authority would be to go against the whole purpose of education, which is to lead, not force, out of darkness of ignorance, frailty, and fear. To restrain ourselves can sometimes be very difficult for us. Out of concern, we want to ensure the better choice. But he who called himself the Way does not. He invites and waits for a response.[7]

To return to the image of the jigsaw, we may know that it is a beautiful picture when complete. But we cannot impose that judgement on others; they must see it with their own eyes. This is a great challenge for catechesis today, particularly where sacramental preparation is concerned and there may be a preoccupation with the number of people receiving the sacraments. Catechesis offers and invites, it does not impose.

8. He took bread, blessed, broke and distributed it

This is the moment when the disciples realise the beauty of the completed jigsaw. Their eyes are opened and they understand that all the Scriptures point to Jesus who breaks bread for them. The encounter, the journey with Jesus leads to the Eucharist where he gives them himself. Companionship, sharing bread, becomes communion. For catechists, all their work leads naturally to the Eucharist, for this celebration is the source and summit of Christian life. The journey leads people to take their place at the table of the Lord with the community that is journeying with them.

9. They spoke with each other

Dominic Ashkar's catechetical principles, like the Emmaus story itself, now focus on the two disciples. Jesus 'had vanished from their sight' for his presence with them is now different. And the disciples look back on their journey with amazement: 'Did not our hearts burn within us as he talked to us on the road and explained the scriptures to us?' (Luke 24:32). 'Now the disciples understood what they had gone through, the meaning of their groping, their searching. The Lord was there all along, but they had not known it. Their faith became solid because of the friendly exchange between themselves and Jesus at each stage of the journey'.[8]

For catechists, this stage of the journey means allowing those catechised to share their story, their understanding of what has happened to them. The journey of faith is not something undertaken as individuals, but within a community. It is right and natural that the searching, the questions and the feelings should be shared. At this stage of the journey the proper question should be: 'How can we use the information and experience of the journey?' It is still a point of departure.

10. They got up immediately and returned to Jerusalem

At the end of Matthew's Gospel, Jesus commissions the disciples to go out and proclaim the Good News, to carry on his work. Having accompanied him throughout his life, a specific task is entrusted to them. Likewise, the disciples who have journeyed to Emmaus return immediately to Jerusalem to tell their good news. They are transformed and cannot wait to share their experience.

> This final scene of Emmaus underscores the fact that when Christians enter a personal relationship with Christ, faith cannot remain individualistic or stay enclosed within a small, close-knit group. Our faith must go beyond; it must bring others into the believing community or, if they are already in it, bring them to the fullness of revelation ... Fulfilled faith puts people on the road because of their urge to share the Good News that they cannot keep to themselves.[9]

Catechesis is about students becoming teachers.

REFLECTION

- What do you think of the Emmaus story as a model for catechesis? Do you find any of the catechetical principles difficult to grasp?

- Dominic Ashkar's principles suggest that the response to Jesus cannot be imposed, that a choice – even if it might be the wrong one – must be left to the individual. How hard is this, particularly in catechesis with young people? What implications do you think this has for first reconciliation, first Eucharist, and confirmation? What sort of choice faces those who are given no example of practising faith?

- '. . . we don't have to be expert theologians like Jesus, nor do our students need to be in despair like the disciples . . . All that the story tells us, all that is required, is that we, like Jesus, keep our students at the point of departure, because as far as they are concerned the most important thing in learning is the teacher and only secondarily the message'.[10] What is your reaction to this statement? What challenges does it lay down for the catechist? Have you any experience of situations where the message is secondary? Do you agree with this statement?

Who is the catechist?

The Emmaus story sees Jesus as Teacher and Catechist. This fact is also reflected in the 1997 *General Directory for Catechesis*, in which Part Three is entitled 'The pedagogy of the faith'. (Pedagogy, a technical term for the science of teaching, comes from a Greek word for education.) In the Introduction to this section it states:

> Jesus gave careful attention to the formation of the disciples whom he sent out on mission. He presented himself to them as the only teacher and, at the same time, a patient and faithful friend. He exercised real teaching 'by means of his whole life' . . . In Jesus Christ, Lord and Teacher, the Church finds transcendent grace, permanent inspiration

and the convincing model for all communication of the faith.[11]

Any reflection on 'Who is the catechist?' must begin, therefore, with the person of Jesus, for he provides the example.

> In his words, signs and works during his brief but intense life, the disciples had direct experience of the fundamental traits of the 'pedagogy of Jesus', and recorded them in the Gospels: receiving others, especially the poor, the little ones and sinners, as persons loved and sought out by God; the undiluted proclamation of the Kingdom of God as the good news of the truth and of the consolation of the Father; a kind of delicate and strong love which liberates from evil and promotes life; a pressing invitation to a manner of living sustained by faith in God, by hope in the Kingdom and by charity to one's neighbour; the use of all the resources of interpersonal communication, such as word, silence, metaphor, image, example, and many diverse signs as was the case with the biblical prophets. Inviting his disciples to follow him unreservedly and without regret, Christ passed on to them his pedagogy of faith as a full sharing in his actions and his destiny.[12]

The *General Directory* points out that the pedagogy of Jesus is, of course, rooted in the pedagogy of God himself, who entrusts words of instruction and catechesis which are transmitted from generation to generation. The Church, too, is a living catechesis, in continuing the mission of the Father and Son through the power of the Holy Spirit.

For the catechist today, then, Jesus Christ remains the primary Teacher and example. This means that first of all the catechist is someone with their own personal relationship with God. Catechists will have their own faith experiences and stories, resulting in awareness of God in their lives. This does not mean that every catechist must be prepared to witness to their faith in a very public, charismatic manner. Awareness of their own unique relationship with God and how that may have changed and developed over the years is the foundation for the ministry of the catechist. To nurture the faith of others depends on catechists having nurtured and reflected on their own faith first.

As we have seen the *General Directory for Catechesis* listed many aspects of the ministry of Jesus as recorded in the Gospels. These aspects must be reflected in the catechist, too, as he or she tries to bring people into communion with Jesus. His way of teaching, though, offers some important considerations for the catechist:

> Jesus never introduced ideas which did not relate to people's lives, which did not connect to an authentic question. He never taught concepts that required a new vocabulary or were related to abstract ideas. Jesus pushed the people to see things differently and act differently in very profound ways, but to do this he appealed to their own experience and helped them to see the manifestation of God in that experience.[13]

The catechist is someone whose primary concern is with people, accompanying them on a journey of faith. It is that ability to journey, to be a companion, which is an essential characteristic of the ministry of catechesis. This must take priority over the ability to impart doctrinal information and means that catechists must know their target audience. The *Catechism of the Catholic Church* makes this point with a direct quote from its predecessor from 1566, the *Roman Catechism*:

> Whoever teaches must become 'all things to all men' (1 Cor. 9:22), to win everyone to Christ . . . Above all, teachers must not imagine that a single kind of soul has been entrusted to them, and that consequently it is lawful to teach and form equally all the faithful in true piety with one and the same method! Let them realize that some are in Christ as newborn babes, others as adolescents, and still others as adults in full command of their powers . . . Those who are called to the ministry of preaching must suit their words to the maturity and understanding of their hearers, as they hand on the teaching of the mysteries of faith and the rules of moral conduct.[14]

Catechists, then, must be aware of what, in modern-day

religious parlance, is often referred to as the stages of faith development. In this everyone is not the same, as the *Roman Catechism* made clear. It is here that the importance of psychological development comes into play.

The catechist should not be overawed by this. It is not a request that every catechist must also be an expert in psychology and the stages of faith development. Rather, it is a basic plea that every catechist must know the target audience and adapt the message accordingly. This may seem to be stating the obvious but it is a fact that is often overlooked. For example, we would never consider doing complicated mathematical sums with a group of five-year-olds. 'Number work' seems to be the more appropriate starting-point. And yet in handing on faith to that same group of young children it could be so easy to rush in at an adult level and hand on lots of religious information. This is perhaps most obvious at the celebration of Mass, where the particular challenge of catechesis with young children is introducing them to what is really an adult celebration using language that, effectively, is not immediately suited to children's age and stage of faith development. Indeed, this bold statement from the 1973 *Directory on Children's Masses* makes interesting reading:

> The church is the place where children should receive a Christian education, but there is a problem here. Liturgical, and especially eucharistic celebrations, which of their very nature have an educative value, are scarcely fully effective where children are concerned. The Mass may be in their own language, but the words and symbols used are not those which they can understand . . . it must surely be spiritually harmful to them to have the experience of going to church for years without ever understanding properly what is going on.[15]

Of course, the suggestion here is *not* that young children should not be present at Mass. But it highlights the challenge of handing on faith in an effective manner. This challenge is not resolved by simply ensuring that young children 'know' their faith, that they know certain things by a certain age. This goes against the whole concept of fidelity to God and fidelity to the person emphasised in many catechetical developments of the twentieth century and in the *General Directory for Catechesis* (cf. n. 55).

Catechesis of adults

It is clear, then, that in working with any group, from adults to young children, the catechist should be aware of some basic ideas concerning faith development and the background of the people within the group. While it is not the role of this book to provide an exhaustive treatise on psychological and faith development, a few important comments are appropriate.

The *General Directory for Catechesis* states that catechesis of adults, which remains the example for all catechesis, 'must take serious account of their experience, of their conditioning and of the challenges which they have encountered in life'.[16] Once again this is the fundamental concept of knowing where people are. As stated before, it is important to have some understanding of how adults learn and know that they must feel comfortable. This is not just a statement about the state of the chairs they might be sitting in, although there is something difficult about trying to run an adult reflection group in a small classroom with the participants sitting on chairs made for seven-year-olds! Adults must feel comfortable with the whole learning process. Irrespective of background and circumstances every adult needs to feel valued and respected. They must feel that they are building on their experiences, not just rejecting the past. And the whole process must seem relevant to daily life, an attempt to integrate faith and life in that essential double fidelity to God and to the person.

The adult is assisted to discover, evaluate and activate what he has received by nature and grace, both in the Christian community and by living in human society; in this way, he will be able to overcome the dangers of standardization and of anonymity which are particularly dominant in some societies of today and which lead to loss of identity and lack of appreciation for the resources and qualities of the individual.[17]

Catechesis must never lose sight of the individual.

Catechesis of young people and children

There is an old joke in which religious ministers of different Christian denominations are talking about a common problem: how to get rid of a flock of birds nesting in the church roof. Various schemes to get rid of the birds, from putting down poison to shooting them, have been tried with no success. However, the Catholic priest, with a broad smile, admits that he has got rid of the birds nesting in the roof of his church. 'It was easy,' he says. 'I confirmed them and haven't seen them since!'

It is often young people who are the focus of great concern as regards handing on faith. The *General Directory for Catechesis* makes this quite clear, calling young people 'the first victims of the spiritual and cultural crisis gripping the world ... Very often at this time the pre-adolescent, in receiving the sacrament of Confirmation, formally concludes the process of Christian initiation but from that moment virtually abandons completely the practice of the faith.'[18]

Youth catechesis must be revised and revitalised. Alienation from the Church or religious indifference is the backdrop of which all catechists must be aware. This may be the result of a lack of religious formation in the home or some sort of peer pressure. The most successful catechesis, as the *General Directory* points out, will be that 'which is given in the context of the wider pastoral care of young people, especially when it addresses the problems affecting their lives'.[19] It is easy to see here how important is the catechetical principle from the Emmaus story which states that one begins by finding out what is important to young people at this moment. There could be nothing more off-putting for young people interested in the latest TV programmes and computer games than to be told to forget all those because they are now starting a lesson on the gifts of the Holy Spirit.

In the context of working with young people, the *General Directory* also makes an important point about language: 'One of the difficulties to be addressed and resolved is the question of "language" (*mentality, sensibility, tastes, style, vocabulary*) between young people and the Church (*catechesis, catechists*). A necessary "adaptation of catechesis to young people" is urged, in order to translate into their terms "the message of Jesus with patience and wisdom and without betrayal" '.[20] While it is important that young people develop a religious literacy it is also essential that religious language be suited to their age and stage of faith development. This is especially true in the matter of prayer. I remember a school Mass with almost two hundred children aged between four and eleven, and in the silence after Communion one of the teachers asked the children to recite the 'Communion aspiration'. In unison they chanted: 'Jesus, Mary, and Joseph, I give you my heart and my soul. Jesus, Mary, and Joseph, assist me in my last agony. Jesus, Mary and Joseph, may I die in peace, and in your blessed company.' Quite what the five-year-olds made of this I don't know. The *General Directory for Catechesis* talks separately of catechesis of infants, young children and young people. This latter category covers pre-adolescence, adolescence and young adulthood. As regards infants and children, the *General Directory* acknowledges that catechesis at this stage is the work of various partners, with particular attention being paid to the role of family and school. 'In a certain sense nothing replaces family catechesis, especially for its positive and receptive environment, for the example of adults, and for its first explicit experience and practice of the faith'.[21] Catechists working with young children must bear in mind this family background. This could present particular challenges if a child comes from a family where there is little example of practice of the faith or explicit religious experience. The Christian community has a clear responsibility here, and must 'provide generous, competent and realistic aid, by seeking dialogue with the families, by proposing appropriate forms of education and by providing catechesis which is proportionate to the concrete possibilities and needs of these children'.[22]

Awareness of family circumstances can also give rise to care with use of religious language. For example, while not denying fundamental beliefs, sensitivity is required regarding frequent reference to God as Father with a child whose experience of fatherhood is not positive. In fact, with children there is the potential to explore many aspects of God – as Father, Mother, Creator, Spirit, Friend, and so on.

With the catechesis of infants and children there can come, too, the challenge of the catechesis of parents. This is especially true at the first celebration of the sacraments of reconciliation and Eucharist. It is becoming more commonplace now to prepare not only the children but also their parents, acknowledging with each group their age and stage of faith development. It is a fact that a child's celebration of these sacraments may often bring parents back to some degree of practice of faith. The same is true of baptism, when the birth of a baby can stimulate parents to rekindle their own faith. Catechists cannot and do not replace parents, but they can help them to fulfil the prayer made at a child's baptism that the parents may be the best of teachers, bearing witness to the faith by what they say and do.

The religious education of children continues in the school environment. It is not limited to a particular lesson but is linked to the entire ethos of the school. Religious education sows the seeds of the gospel. It must

> appear as a scholastic discipline with the same systematic demands and the same rigour as other disciplines. It must present the Christian message and the Christian event with the same seriousness and the same depth with which other disciplines present their knowledge. It should not be an accessory alongside of these disciplines, but rather it should engage in a necessary inter-disciplinary dialogue ... Through inter-disciplinary dialogue religious instruction in schools underpins, activates, develops and completes the educational activity of the school.[23]

Given the different backgrounds of children that has already been noted, some children will receive religious education as evangelisation, hearing the Good News possibly for the first time; others will receive it as catechesis, deepening the personal relationship with God on which their faith is based. Thus, religious education and catechesis remain distinct yet complementary.[24]

REFLECTION

• What aspects of Jesus the Teacher appeal to you the most? How could a catechist use some of his methods today?

• 'Unless we have an appreciation of how people develop and learn at different stages of life, we may present the Christian tradition in ways which are unsuited to their ability and irrelevant to their experiences and needs'.[25] Choose one group – children, young people, or adults – and reflect on the physical, intellectual, social, emotional, moral and religious factors which would need to be taken into account in handing on faith.

• Think of any time you may have spoken about religious matters with another adult. How easy was it? What do you think are some of the most important elements of working with adults?

• Some parents have been known to tell their teenage children that they have to go to church because 'I had to when I was your age'. What sort of image of faith does that transmit? How might a catechist begin to work with teenagers? What do you think interests them?

• 'The church is the place where children should receive a Christian education, but there is a problem here. Liturgical, and especially eucharistic celebrations, which of their very nature have an educative value, are scarcely fully effective where children are concerned. The Mass may be in their own language, but the words and symbols used are not those which they can understand ... it must surely be spiritually harmful to them to have the experience of going to church for years without ever understanding properly what is going on'.[26] For pre-adolescent children which aspects of the Mass are understandable, which are not? How can an adult celebration be made more nourishing for children? How can the Mass be 'spiritually harmful'?

• 'No greater disservice could be done to Religion in this country than that religious education in schools should be the half-hearted communication of half-comprehended truths by the half-trained to the half-interested' (A.G. Wedderspoon, 1964). What do you think?

Catechesis: sources and resources

The 1990 document *Adult Catechesis in the Christian Community* was clear in outlining the points of reference for adult catechesis. It

> makes explicit in the life of adults the reality of God's message . . . it goes to the core of the doctrinal content of our Catholic faith, presenting the fundamental beliefs of the creed in a way that relates to the life experience of people, instilling in them a faith mentality; it calls for a structured and organized, though perhaps very elementary, faith journey, which is expressed and sustained by listening to the Word of God, by celebration (liturgy), by charitable service (diakonia), and by a forthright witness in the various situations in which adults find themselves.[27]

The *General Directory for Catechesis* sees catechesis as rooted in the Word of God contained in Scripture and Tradition and interpreted in the Church's teaching (Magisterium).[28]

For the catechist this calls for a certain familiarity with Scripture and the Church's teaching. The Bible is a primary source of catechesis for all age groups. For catechists, it is a challenge to communicate the Bible as a *living* text, not as an old book written a long time ago. A diocesan liturgical commission once criticised those priests and deacons who committed what it called the sin of 'bibliolatry', raising the Book of the Gospels to say 'This is the Gospel of the Lord'. The argument was that it is just a book published by a particular publisher, while the Gospel of the Lord is a living text! Aside from the liturgical niceties, the point is important. The Bible is a living text, a text whose message is one of hope for today. It is this which the catechist must communicate and any formation for catechists must take this into account:

> Besides being a witness, the catechist must also be a teacher who teaches the faith. A biblico-theological formation should afford the catechist an organic awareness of the Christian message, structured around the central mystery of the faith, Jesus Christ . . . In its own level of theological

instruction, the doctrinal content of the formation of a catechist is that which the catechist must transmit. For its
part, 'Sacred Scripture should be the very soul of this formation'.[29]

The mention of doctrinal content brings to mind the *Catechism
of the Catholic Church*. What is the role of such a book in parish
catechesis? A number of different responses can be made to
this question. There will be those who think the publication of
the *Catechism* was a step backwards, a return to an old way
of thinking, while there will be others who think that it was
the answer to lots of prayers. So just where does the *Catechism*
fit into parish catechesis?

The American Archbishop of Milwaukee, Rembert G. Weakland OSB, expressed the role of the *Catechism* quite succinctly in
a book foreword: 'Every catechist', he wrote, 'should be armed
with that *Catechism of the Catholic Church* and refer to it frequently. But it remains a reference tool, too large for any
catechist to absorb or synthesize totally. Nor can one teach from
it, as useful as it may be'.[30] He was echoing the *General Directory
for Catechesis* which had stated that the *Catechism* 'remains the
fundamental doctrinal reference point together with the catechism proper to the particular Church'.[31] For the catechist,
then, the *Catechism* is a useful tool. It is a reference book, not a
textbook.

The importance to catechesis of Scripture and the *Catechism*
are amply reflected in the *General Directory for Catechesis*, which
refers to Scripture and Tradition as sources of catechesis:

> Sacred Scripture, as 'the word of God written under the
> inspiration of the Holy Spirit', and the *Catechism of the Cath-
> olic Church*, as a significant contemporary expression of the
> living Tradition of the Church and a sure norm for teaching
> the faith, are called, each in its own way and according to
> its specific authority, to nourish catechesis in the Church
> of today . . . Both Sacred Scripture and the *Catechism of the
> Catholic Church* must inform biblical as well as doctrinal
> catechesis so that they become true vehicles of the content
> of God's word. In the ordinary development of catechesis
> it is important that catechumens and those to be catechized

can have trust in both Sacred Scripture and the local catechism. Catechesis, by definition, is nothing other than the living and meaningful transmission of these 'documents of faith'.[32]

Prayer and the catechist

But reliance on texts must not hide the fundamental importance of prayer. A distinction already acknowledged in this text is that between what is often termed 'head' faith and 'heart' faith, between an intellectual approach to or understanding of the faith and a view of faith as a unique, personal relationship with God and others (and, of course, there is the further aspect of 'hands faith', referring to the effect that faith has on daily life). The former – head faith – is the content of Revelation and the gospel, the faith which is believed, the *fides quae*. The latter, faith seen as adherence to God who reveals himself, is a personal commitment to a relationship, the faith by which one believes, the *fides qua*. It is this which is rooted in prayer and calls the catechist to be first of all a person of prayer.

It is significant that a number of experts encouraged people to begin reading the *Catechism of the Catholic Church* at Part Four, on Christian Prayer. This was not so that they could find answers or definitions, but so that they could begin to experience how people have prayed. 'Introducing people to prayer and doing so within our rich and broad Catholic tradition is a major task of the entire church family and of catechists in particular, in order to respond to one of the primary hungers of people, illustrated so vividly in the Gospel story when one of the disciples approached Jesus and asked him, "Lord, teach us to pray" (Lk. 11:1)'.[33]

There is an important distinction to be made here between prayer and piety. The catechist is called to share the struggles and pains of prayer, not simply to encourage the trappings of piety. Prayer can be difficult, it can be frustrating. The catechist is called to witness to the reality of prayer, to be, above all, a person of profound faith who has experienced the struggles of daily prayer: 'We pray as we live, because we live as we pray.

If we do not want to act habitually according to the Spirit of Christ, neither can we pray habitually in his name. The "spiritual battle" of the Christian's new life is inseparable from the battle of prayer'.[34] Prayer must reflect life, which is itself full of joys and sorrows.

Of course it is important that the catechist witnesses to prayer not just as a struggle. Prayer is, first of all, an awareness that God has taken the initiative, that he is interested in every human being: 'For Zion was saying, "Yahweh has abandoned me, the Lord has forgotten me"'. Does a woman forget her baby at the breast, or fail to cherish the son of her womb? Yet even if these forget, I will never forget you. See, I have branded you on the palms of my hands' (Isaiah 49:14–16a). The response to this is one of praise and thanksgiving, and so the catechist is called to witness that prayer is first of all a response of praise and thanksgiving. So often it can seem to be limited to prayer of intercession, asking God for this or that. On a serious level this seems to forget the challenging words of the Our Father, where it is said 'Your will be done'. Indeed, I remember in seminary asking my spiritual director if God always answered prayer. 'Yes,' he said, 'only sometimes the answer might be "No".' On a lighter note, it would be good to remember the saying that 'God gave us two ears and one mouth, to be used in those proportions'!

The catechist is not called to be a saint who spends hours and hours in perfect contemplation of God. But the catechist *is* called to hand on faith, not mere information, and that faith must be rooted in personal prayer. With infants and young children, there can sometimes be the complaint that 'They don't know their prayers'. I would suggest that the task of the catechist, working with any group from infants to adults, is not just that of handing on the word-order of certain formal texts. These texts are good, but only if they can be used in the context of a relationship with God, a relationship of prayer first and prayers second. Above all, the catechist must be a person of prayer.

The role of the praying catechist is not to impose one way of prayer. It is not a question of 'It worked for me, therefore it will work for you', and neither is it a question of the catechist

needing to reveal his or her deepest spiritual experiences. These
are personal and cannot be imposed on others. But the catechist
must open others to the fundamental nature of prayer as a
relationship with God. While the expression of that relationship
is personal, the catechist may be able to explore some ways of
prayer, such as communal prayer, charismatic prayer, a leaning
towards popular, pious devotion, meditation, and formal and
spontaneous prayer.

The disciples, those closest to Jesus, said 'Lord, teach us to
pray'. Those who lived and walked with him acknowledged
their own spiritual need. Today, the catechist can offer some
insight into this fundamental spiritual need.

REFLECTION

- '...it is a question of forming catechists for the need to
  evangelize in the present historical context, with its values,
  challenges and disappointments. To accomplish this task, it
  is necessary for catechists to have a deep faith, a clear
  Christian and ecclesial identity, as well as a great social sensitivity'.[35] How important are these characteristics? How can
  they help the catechist accomplish the task of handing on
  faith?

- 'If catechesis is about bringing the good news of God's salvific love to any age group and under any circumstance, I
  suggest three attributes catechists need if they are to carry
  out this ministry effectively: a profound faith, a sound formation, and an ability to adapt'.[36] Think about these three
  attributes. What importance do you attach to each? Can you
  see them in yourself?

- How would you begin to talk to someone about prayer?
  What is your own daily experience of prayer?

- Definitions of prayer vary from the formal 'raising of the
  mind and heart to God' to the simple 'conversation with
  God'. What definitions or writings about prayer have helped
  you?

- 'When I pray, I pray quickly because I'm talking to God. But
  when I read the Bible, I read slowly because God's talking

to me' (anon.). What do you think of this saying? How can
the Bible be useful in prayer? How would you talk about
'praying the Bible'?

7 Some Pastoral Concerns

There is a wonderful cartoon showing two children standing with Spot, the dog. One of the children proudly declares, 'I taught Spot how to whistle.' The other child moves closer to Spot and says, 'I can't hear him whistling.' 'I said I taught him,' comes the reply, 'I didn't say he learned.'

One of the many pastoral concerns with catechesis today is precisely trying to achieve this balance between teaching and learning. How, if at all, can we be sure that what catechists hand on is actually received? How can we be sure that what is being done really makes a difference? In short, the theory is wonderful, the Emmaus story convincing, but what about the reality of catechesis in the daily life of the parish?

The parish as an environment for catechesis

The parish is 'the "privileged place" where "catechesis is realized not only through formal instruction, but also in the liturgy, sacraments and charitable activity" '.[1] *On Catechesis in our Time* is more specific, saying that

> every big parish or every group of parishes has the serious duty to train people completely dedicated to providing catechetical leadership (priests, men and women religious, and lay people), to provide the equipment needed for catechesis under all aspects, to increase and adapt the places for catechesis to the extent that it is possible and useful to do so, and to be watchful about the quality of the religious formation of the various groups and their integration into the ecclesial community.[2]

Catechesis does not occur in some form of isolation. It right-fully takes place within the context of a parish community. That the parish is the pre-eminent place for catechesis is an important fact to grasp and implies a shift in the understanding of how and who hands on faith. The term 'religious education/instruction' suggests a model of handing on faith based on some sort of formal teaching. In effect it is a school model of handing on faith. 'Catechesis' implies a different model, rooted in the parish community. This involves all parishioners, not just one person instructing another.

> Catechetical pedagogy will be effective to the extent that the Christian community becomes a point of concrete refer-ence for the faith journey of individuals. This happens when the community is proposed as a source, *locus* and means of catechesis. Concretely, the community becomes a visible place of faith–witness. It provides for the formation of its members. It receives them as the family of God. It constitutes itself as the living and permanent environment for growth in the faith.[3]

A simple example about the parish environment highlights the effectiveness or otherwise of witness in and by a parish community. I remember a lady attending a particular parish church, which was not her own, every Sunday for nearly two months, searching for some spiritual comfort. At the end of that time she wrote to the parish priest to express her gratitude for what she had experienced. However, she also noted how sad it was that in those two months not one person had spoken to her. To this day I wonder what image of the parish as a caring community, reaching out to all individuals, she went away with. Indeed, the Archbishop of Milwaukee, Rembert Weakland osb, once said: 'The grand model of church in the United States today is McDonald's: self-service, cheap prices, eat fast, and get out. There is no need for community'. And that image need not be limited to the United States.

This story is a reminder of the four fundamental elements of catechesis: it is *God's Word* which is proclaimed in and by the *parish community*, leading to active participation in the *liturgical life* of the community, and having outreach into some aspect of *service* in the community.

It is useful at this stage to make a distinction between what is often called 'formal' and 'informal' catechesis. Formal catechesis refers to those organised, structured sessions which are often associated with sacramental preparation for all age groups. Informal catechesis covers many aspects of handing on faith which are not so tightly structured and sometimes even less overtly religious. This could include such factors as the witness of the community, the social interaction of the community, and the degree to which all members of the community exercise some aspect of welcome to the community.

Catechesis within the parish environment calls for some sort of training for those who are going to undertake this important ministry. Particularly in its more formal aspects catechesis does not just happen and catechists do not just appear. Nor should it just be a situation of 'helping Father'. If a parish is serious about handing on faith, catechists must be trained, not presumed or used because 'Father' wants them. Furthermore, is the decision to train catechists stimulated by a date in the parish diary (or even the bishop's diary) or by an acknowledgement of the continual call to hand on faith? Although situations and resources vary from diocese to diocese, all that is possible should be done to facilitate the training of catechists. The *General Directory for Catechesis* mentions the importance of both basic training and ongoing formation. This could be interpreted as suggesting that it is desirable to move away from a model of catechesis which offers limited training for catechists simply for specific sacramental programmes. Ongoing formation would suggest that the role of catechists is not over once the sacramental programme has ended or the sacrament has been celebrated. In referring to the role of the diocese, the *General Directory* states that

> diocesan pastoral programmes must give absolute priority to the *formation of lay catechists*. Together with this, a fundamentally decisive element must be the *catechetical formation of priests* both at the level of seminary formation as well as at the level of continuing formation. Bishops are called

upon to ensure that they are scrupulously attentive to such formation.[4]

A serious challenge indeed.

Training for catechists

So if this training is so important, what should it entail? 'Formation seeks to enable catechists to transmit the Gospel to those who desire to entrust themselves to Jesus Christ. The purpose of formation, therefore, is to make the catechist capable of communicating: "The summit and centre of catechetical formation lies in an aptitude and ability to communicate the Gospel message" '.[5]

One of the fundamental elements in training catechists is ensuring that they have this aptitude and ability to communicate. The skills necessary for communication cannot be presumed. While it can be easy to find experts on a particular religious theme, it is more difficult to find experts who can also communicate their expertise in an intelligible manner. Likewise with catechists. One of the most important skills they must have is that of being able to communicate. This implies knowing their target audience and being able to adapt their message to that audience. It also says something important about language, for language is more than a form of communication. It is a way of reaching the hearts and minds of people, calling for sincerity and simplicity.

The following story says so much about the ability to communicate, know your target audience, and use the right language. A parish priest was in the habit of going into the primary school each Monday to talk to the children, aged up to eight or nine. The setting was always formal, and the priest realised that a lot of the children he saw in school he rarely saw in church. Furthermore, their responses to his religious questions were none too good. So he decided on a new approach. On Monday morning he went into the classroom, sat the children on the floor in front of him, and he perched on the corner of the desk. 'Now children,' he began, 'can anyone tell me what is small, grey, and has a big bushy tail?' Absolute silence. And then a little boy spoke up: 'Well, Father,' he said, 'I know the answer *should* be Jesus but it sounds like a squirrel to me.' This says so much about the ability to adapt!

What the catechist is being trained to do is clearly expressed by the *General Directory*:

> This aim is nothing other than to lead the catechist to know how to animate a catechetical journey of which the necessary stages are: the proclamation of Jesus Christ; making known his life by setting it in the context of salvation history; explanation of the mystery of the Son of God, made man for us; and finally to help the catechumen, or those being catechized, to identify with Jesus Christ through the sacraments of initiation. With continuing catechesis, the catechist merely tries to deepen these basic elements.[6]

If formation for catechists is about enabling them to transmit the gospel, or animate a catechetical journey, what elements should it contain? As noted already, the obvious starting-point is ensuring that catechists have an ability to communicate. This raises the question: what is to be communicated? Here the focus moves more directly to the content of the catechist's work.

The teacher teaches the faith. That message must be focused first of all on the person of Jesus Christ and must be biblically-based. The catechist should be familiar with the Bible. This may seem an obvious statement to make, but for some Roman Catholics it can appear almost revolutionary. As we have seen in the history of catechesis, the Bible was often used simply as a proof-text, justifying a particular opinion. Biblical scholarship was, for a long time, frowned upon and reading of the Bible was not positively encouraged. How times have changed:

> The explanation of the Word of God in *catechesis* has Sacred Scripture as first source. Explained in the context of the Tradition, Scripture provides the starting-point, foundation and norm of catechetical teaching. One of the goals of catechesis should be to initiate a person in a correct understanding and fruitful reading of the Bible. This will bring about the discovery of the divine truth it contains and

evoke as generous a response as is possible to the message God addresses through his word to the whole human race ... The presentation of the Gospels should be done in such a way as to elicit an encounter with Christ, who provides the key to the whole biblical revelation and communicates the call of God that summons each one to respond. The word of the prophets and that of the "ministers of the Word" (Luke 1:2) ought to appear as something addressed to Christians now.[7]

The catechist is not called to be an expert Scripture scholar armed with degrees in biblical languages. But the catechist *is* called to be familiar with the Scriptures both on an intellectual and a personal level. To be able to share what the Scriptures mean on a personal, daily level is the very process of re-echoing the gospel. It is not simply a matter of interpreting texts, but the ability to interpret the 'signs of the times' and show how those texts are important and relevant today. The catechist must be a person for whom the Bible is a source of strength and prayer in daily life.

Another aspect of the catechist's ministry of handing on faith concerns the teaching of the Church. In working especially with adults, a recurring question can often be, 'What does the Church teach about ...?' Once again, the catechist should not be overawed by this and presume that what is required is an encyclopaedic knowledge of the Catholic faith. The *Catechism of the Catholic Church* is a useful reference point in this regard, but again the *General Directory for Catechesis* leans more towards the catechist's personal assimilation of the truths of faith:

> This synthesis of faith should be such as to help the catechist to mature in his own faith and enable him to offer an explanation for the present hope in this time of mission: 'The situation today points to an ever-increasing urgency for doctrinal formation of the lay faithful, not simply for a better understanding which is natural to faith's dynamism, but also in enabling them to "give a reason for their hope" in view of the world and its grave and complex problems'.[8]

The key here is the catechist's ability to express what personal difference the doctrinal truths of faith mean in daily life. This idea was once memorably expressed by the late Cardinal George Basil Hume (1923–99) in an explicit reference to catechesis with young people: 'Young people today,' he said, 'do not want to know what we believe; they want to know what it means to us. If we communicate that, then they begin to want it to mean something to them.' Once again, the link between witness and belief is inseparable.

The training of catechists must also include what the *General Directory* calls the 'human sciences': 'In pastoral care sufficient use should be made, not only of theological principles, but also of secular findings, especially in the fields of psychology and sociology: in this way the faithful will be brought to a more mature living of the faith'.[9] Just as the earlier emphasis on adequate theological preparation did not imply that every catechist needs a theology degree, so likewise the emphasis on use of the human sciences does not suggest that every catechist must also be a psychologist. The *General Directory* says that catechists should know something about what motivates people, about the human life-cycle and personality structure, and be able to examine some of the sociological, economic and cultural conditions which influence people today. Such a list should not strike fear into the heart of every catechist! Rather, it is surely just a concrete application of that basic principle of 'knowing your target audience'. To really know them means to understand what motivates them, what background they come from.

This is essential information when deciding what technique to use in catechesis:

> The catechist is an educator who facilitates maturation of the faith which catechumens and those being catechized obtain with the help of the Holy Spirit ... Formation seeks to mature an educational capacity in the catechist which implies: an ability to be attentive to people, an ability to interpret or respond to educational tasks or initiatives in organizing learning activities and the ability of leading a human group towards maturity.[10]

Again, this should not be seen as a daunting ideal. It is a

call for catechists to appreciate and understand their role as educators. Indeed, in many parish situations it is often presumed that the catechists will be schoolteachers. Although teachers might also be good as catechists, the ability to teach in a classroom should not be equated with the ability to catechise. It is important, though, that the catechist has some understanding of how people learn, how groups work, and what teaching techniques can be used to draw out of people the seed of faith sown in them. A simple example may suffice. You may remember, in reflecting on the history of catechesis, that an important technique some centuries ago was the use of pictures, stained glass windows and statues. It was a visual way of handing on faith to many people who could not read. Children, and indeed many adults, love drawing. With children the drawing of biblical stories can help to bring that story to life for a young age group. Most adults would not expect to be asked to paint their favourite Bible story! Hence, the importance of different techniques. Reflection on the Bible at an adult level would be approached in a very different way, but what is common in working with both adults and children is the centrality of the Word.

Catechists should not think that so far they have been asked to accumulate a degree in theology and biblical studies, a diploma in psychology, and now a masters in the philosophy and techniques of modern education! Being aware of different learning methods and techniques for teaching is again a simple extension of knowing your target audience. Knowing them implies knowing what works with them. It is putting into practice that well-known Chinese proverb: 'Tell me and I forget. Show me and I remember. Involve me and I understand.' Catechesis is about involving.

REFLECTION

- What catechesis is going on in your parish? Is it formal or informal? How is it prepared for and how is the whole of the community involved?
- The parish is a privileged place for catechesis. How wel-

coming is your parish? Who are the catechists? How are they trained? What ongoing formation takes place?

• 'At the heart of catechesis we find, in essence, a Person, the Person of Jesus of Nazareth, the only Son from the Father . . . To catechize is "to reveal in the Person of Christ the whole of God's eternal design reaching fulfilment in that Person . . ." '.[11] How can a catechist begin to reveal the person of Jesus Christ? Is Jesus Christ central to the person of the catechist?

• How central to the daily life of a catechist is the Bible? Does a catechist have to read it every day?

• A child is not a reduced model of an adult. What do you think are the catechetical implications of such a statement?

FAQs or Qs & As

This heading is not an indication that the author has introduced some strange shorthand, but the ever-more common acronyms for 'Frequently Asked Questions' (FAQs) and 'Questions and Answers' (Qs & As). So here goes!

Why should I be a catechist?

A catechist is someone who has an adult faith and can lead others on a journey of faith. That is the basic idea. Other skills can be developed in the course of the journey, for the catechist, too, is making a journey of faith. So, in one sense everyone can be, indeed should be, a catechist.

But I'm not worthy and I'm not very intelligent.

A catechist is not someone who is superior to or above other people. Being a catechist is not about being worthy or unworthy, clever or not so clever. It is about wanting to spread the Good News, to carry on the work that Jesus began.

So what do I have to do?

A catechist is not someone working in isolation. It is a person working in and on behalf of a parish community, carrying out an important service of the Word. This task must be fulfilled with enthusiasm. So, first of all be enthusiastic! A catechist then needs to be adequately formed for the ministry. It is the duty of priests to ensure that catechesis is well structured and oriented. Furthermore, the priest should discern vocations to the service of catechesis. It is his role, then, to ensure that those catechists who have said 'Yes' to the call to lead others to faith in Jesus Christ are properly trained. So, be open to being a catechist.

So who does the training?

Each parish and diocese should have effective training courses available. The bishop must ensure effective priority is given to catechesis, by putting into operation the necessary personnel, means, equipment and financial resources. He is also called on to establish an articulated, coherent and global programme in the diocese in order to respond to the true needs of the people. The parish priest should be able to use a diocesan programme and help catechists in his parish to become co-operators with the programme.

So once I'm trained, that's it? Do I get a certificate?

The question of a certificate is secondary! What is important is that training is not the end of the matter, for catechists should also have ongoing formation to enable them to continue to develop and mature spiritually. There should be regular retreats and input for catechists themselves, so that 'being trained as a catechist' does not become something that is just ticked off on a checklist! Training does not complete the task.

Someone said I have to teach like Jesus. What does that mean?

Jesus was the supreme catechist. He cared for the people he was with, he didn't just fill them with facts. He respected them as individuals, never once stripping them of their dignity or making them feel as if they were second-class citizens. He could do this because of his own deep relationship in prayer with his Father which made it possible for him to hand on what his Father had taught him. Jesus was also open, and people felt that they could come to him and trust him. He never ceased to be about his Father's business; he was enthusiastic to spread the Good News. And when this seemed difficult, he persevered; he did not give up when the first difficulties arose, when the first hint of opposition surfaced.

What do I do if there is opposition, if people disagree with me?

Change, which catechesis inevitably implies, is never easy. Cardinal John Henry Newman (1801–90) wrote: 'To live is to change and to be perfect is to have changed often.'[12] But this is not easy. The catechist will come across people for whom change is very difficult, or who hold preconceived ideas. A simple example: some years ago I spent an evening with a parish group introducing the *Catechism of the Catholic Church*, and at the end of the evening a parishioner stood up and said, 'Father, we've spent a whole evening on the *Catechism* and you haven't once mentioned transubstantiation.' The view expressed there could not conceive of a catechesis which did not begin and end with some treatment of transubstantiation, that any understanding of Catholic doctrine and practice begins and ends with this teaching. Working in a situation where such views are expressed can be difficult. It is also a challenge because the catechist must be one who listens, rather than one who imposes one view in place of another. Working with those who are not open to change is a call to dialogue, not to a shouting match. The conclusion may simply be to agree to disagree, but the catechist must not feel that it is a question of winning or losing. Catechesis is not a competition.

But agreeing to disagree is failure, isn't it? Shouldn't I always be trying to bring people with me? How will I know if I've succeeded?

In truth, you may never know if you've succeeded. To approach catechesis in that way is to approach it with some sort of tickbox mentality. The whole idea of catechesis is summed up in this wonderful story. A woman dreamed that she was in a shop, browsing, looking along the shelves, when she suddenly realised that the assistant behind the counter was God. 'What can I buy here?' she asked him. 'Anything you want,' God replied. 'Well,' the lady said, 'I would like peace, love, joy, wisdom, for everyone throughout the world for ever.' God smiled. 'I think you've got the wrong shop, my dear. We don't sell fruits here, only seeds.' Catechesis is about sowing seeds.

What resources are available to help me do this?

There are many resources, but first of all remember that catechesis is not simply about using the most up-to-date textbooks. The first resource must be the catechist's own life of prayer, a relationship with God rooted in prayer. Trust in his Spirit is at the heart of catechesis, for the catechist who is drawing people to faith is also on that same journey of faith, and the sustenance for that journey is the nourishment provided by God. Following on from this, another resource is life itself, which can provide many insights into the joy and hope, grief and anguish of the journey towards God.

If life is a resource, is that where I start? And doesn't that mean it will be different for everybody?

There is always a tension between the ordinary things in daily life and what some people would call the 'real content' of handing on faith, the doctrines and dogmas of the Church. The

Second Vatican Council's *Pastoral Constitution on the Church in the Modern World* called on the people of God 'to discern the true signs of God's presence and purpose in the events, the needs and the desires which it shares with the rest of humanity today. For faith casts a new light on everything and makes known the full ideal which God has set for humanity'.[13] God communicates through daily life and so daily life is not to be separated from catechesis – it is an inseparable part of it. Indeed, if catechesis is the process whereby the gospel is re-echoed in daily life, or of examining the relationship between life experiences and faith, then it is clear that these experiences must be part of the catechetical process.

Of course, this does not mean to say that catechesis must always *begin* with experience. It can even be argued that to teach in exactly the same way all the time could quickly lead to boredom. There will be times, and it will vary depending on the theme being explored and the nature of the target audience, when it is right to begin with experience and then proceed to examine how that experience may, for example, have echoes in the gospel and in the Church's tradition and teaching. However, there will be other times when it may be useful to begin with what the Church teaches and believes, and then proceed to see how that has echoes in daily life and makes a difference to the way Christians live today.

Catechesis requires a balance. It should be concerned with making people 'attentive to their more significant experiences, both personal and social; it also has the duty of placing under the light of the Gospel, the questions which arise from those experiences';[14] ' . . . a catechesis which inspires not only intellectual assimilation of the faith, but also touches the heart and transforms conduct is correct. Catechesis, thus, generates a dynamic life which is unified by the faith. It bridges the gap between belief and life, between the Christian message and the cultural context and brings forth the fruits of true holiness'.[15]

If experience is so important, then how do I teach doctrine? And if people are wanting to become Catholics, can't I presume they know a certain amount anyway?

First of all, and it might be fairly blunt to say so, it is wrong to presume any content on behalf of those being catechised. This is not out of an attitude of superiority but of realism. For example, an adult may just be inquiring because of a religious experience, without much awareness of the content of belief, while, at the other extreme, a child may come from a particular background where there is little handing on of the content and practice of religious belief.

In teaching doctrine no opposition should be set up between doctrine and life, which the above question seems to imply. Their separation is artificial. To separate the two, or, for example, to have a purely doctrine-led approach, could lead to people thinking that their life experiences are of no worth. The *General Directory for Catechesis* talks about the principle of 'fidelity to God and fidelity to man', emphasising their correlation and interaction.[16]

The place of doctrine in this interaction is not a secondary one. There are basic doctrines of the Church which must be handed on, no matter how uncomfortable they might seem to some listeners. In reading the 'signs of the times' the Church is asked to interpret its teachings for the world of today, not water them down or compromise them in any way so that they might be more palatable to a world whose values may be different. Just as experience is part of the catechetical process, so is doctrine. In Catholic schools in England and Wales, for example, this has been reflected in two recent publications from the Bishops' Conference entitled *What Are We To Teach?* and *Religious Education Curriculum Directory for Catholic Schools*. Both these publications state what the bishops would like taught in Religious Education in Catholic schools, but they do not refer to the methodology. They are about the 'what', not the 'how', but their publication acknowledges that the two are inseparable. At any level in catechesis, doctrine is the essential 'what' of the process, with the 'how' being a variable dependent on a number of other factors.

It is permissible to begin with God to arrive at Christ, and vice versa; similarly, it is permissible to begin with humanity to arrive at God, and vice versa. A method of pedagogy must be chosen in the light of the situation of the ecclesial community or the individual believers to be catechised. Hence the necessity of being at pains to discover the method best suited to each situation.[17]

If doctrine is that important, how do I express it? How sensitive do I have to be? For example, do I *really* have to call God 'Mother'?

Knowing doctrine is one thing, knowing how to teach it is another. A number of basic points should be kept in mind: the role of the catechist is to bring a person into communion with the person of Jesus Christ, and therefore catechesis is, first of all, 'christocentric', to use the posh theological term. This means that catechesis must put a person in touch with what the Church believes and teaches about Jesus Christ, rather than an individual's personal opinion about him.

How all this is done is key, for it is important to show that the Church's doctrines are not, as some might hold, outdated ideas, but essential truths relevant to the world of today. The example offered in the question, about the need to teach about God as Mother, is a good one. Whatever is taught must respect the particular culture, language and social conditions in which it is expressed. How to teach doctrine is a simple application of the principle of knowing your target audience. To return to the example in the question, there are many Old Testament images that portray a maternal side to God, someone who cares, and in catechesis such an emphasis must not be omitted. Again, adapt the message to the target audience, without watering it down or compromising it.

Experience, doctrine, now what about prayer. Do I have to teach something about how to pray?

How empty catechesis would be if it just revealed that experience was valid and that it was linked with doctrine. For all catechesis is directed towards a relationship with God rooted in worship and prayer. It has already been noted that the first word for a catechist must be that of witness, and this includes the witness of prayer. For example, it is often said today that one of the first requisites for a priest is that he may be a man of prayer, that it is a powerful witness, for example, if parishioners see a priest kneeling in prayer before the start of Mass. He is not just appearing to provide a service, but is celebrating a deep, personal relationship with God. Likewise, for the catechist it is a powerful witness that what is shared is some understanding of prayer, not just the right words in the right order, irrespective of the spirit in which they might be said.

It is often said that the role of the catechist is not so much to teach prayers as to introduce people to experiences of prayer. This latter phrase, 'experiences of prayer', covers many things. These include formal prayers, but also silence, using passages from the Bible as prayers ('praying the Bible'), reflection on the Psalms, techniques of meditation, and the whole notion of spontaneous prayer. It is the role of the catechist not to say which is right and which is wrong, which works and which does not, but to offer as many experiences as possible which deepen a personal relationship with God.

An important concept to bear in mind, though, once again relates to the target audience. In as far as is possible, the catechist must be aware of the spiritual capabilities of the group or individuals with whom he or she is working. There is a big difference between knowing words and knowing their meaning. The role of the catechist is surely that of encouraging people to pray, not just to know prayers. To know prayers does not necessarily mean that a person is praying. One is about words in the right order, the other is about a unique, personal relationship.

Experience, doctrine, prayer. So how do I start the discussion?

Even before you start, know what your aim is, or, to put it another way, begin with the end in mind. Adults, in particular, learn better if they have some sense of direction, if they are aware of what they are doing. There is also an important distinction to be made between 'discussion' and 'faith-sharing'. Some parishes advertise 'Talks on the Catholic Faith' as if people are being invited to a series of lectures. That is not the aim of catechesis. So be aware of what people are coming to.

Discussion groups are concerned with opinions, ideas, with what people *think*; some opinions can be right and others wrong. Faith-sharing groups deal with *life*, where people are invited to share aspects of their human and spiritual life-story. For example, a question to be used in a discussion group could be 'why is the Catholic Church the true Church?' In a faith-sharing group the question would be 'why are you still a Catholic?' The second question can only be answered personally.[18]

But won't people shy away from faith-sharing? Isn't faith personal?

Faith is, indeed, personal, and for some people faith-sharing may be an entirely foreign idea. The catechist must be very sensitive. Nobody should be forced to share or be seen as a lesser person because they might not share. Remember, the best witness a catechist can offer is the sharing of his or her own faith. Invite them to share and they might feel called to do so. Sharing will work well if from the outset the catechist fosters a spirit of mutual understanding and trust in the group.

But can I really be a confident catechist?

The simple answer is 'Yes'. You will sow, they will reap. Always bear in mind that you are performing an important ministry of the Word. If you think you are getting nowhere, remember you are sowing seeds, not reaping fruits, and it is important to let God work through you. Of course, there is nothing more guaranteed to destroy your confidence than looking at rows of blank faces, people who seem as if they would much rather be elsewhere or simply don't understand. This is not something new. Read carefully St Augustine's advice from nearly fifteen hundred years ago:

> It is hard to speak on to the end of what you planned to say if you see a listener is not responding – he might be afraid, in such sacred matters, to differ in words or bodily reaction, or he may not grasp or approve what he is being told. Since we cannot see into his mind, we must use words to get a response from that mind, to lure it from its hiding place ... We should wake him up, mentally, with some catchy witticism (fitted to the subject), or bring up something odd and astonishing, perhaps something scary and depressing, preferably having to do with him personally, so self-interest will stimulate him. Yet use no severity; ease him into candor.[19]

What a vision of inculturation, taking people where they are at!

So, what next?

For those in leadership roles, the answer is clear: encourage catechesis, plan for it and make it the priority that many Church documents believe it to be. Handing on faith is not just setting up a sacramental programme but is a daily task rooted in the life of the parish community. Catechesis must not be haphazard.

For those called to hand on faith in the ministry of catechesis, take courage from St Augustine's vision of this work as a service of love, so that by your words people may believe, and hope, and love. And in this way, the path will be prepared for fulfilling the vision expressed by Pope John Paul II in the document *The Vocation and the Mission of the Lay Faithful in the Church and in the World*:

> The eyes of faith behold a wonderful scene: that of a countless number of lay people, both women and men, busy at work in their daily life and activity, oftentimes far from view and quite unacclaimed by the world, unknown to the world's great personages but nonetheless looked upon in love by the Father, untiring labourers who work in the Lord's vineyard. Confident and steadfast through the

power of God's grace, these are the humble yet great builders of the Kingdom of God in history.[20]

So, when you're asked to be a catechist:

> . . . *to impart such instruction,*
> *it will not suffice*
> *to place a small manual in one's hand;*
> *rather it will be necessary*
> *to enkindle a great zeal in one's heart.*

St Augustine, *Enchiridion*, n. 6, written *c.* 421

REFLECTION

- 'Today, using the resources of Vatican II and our own insights, we are called to excite people about being part of an alive, dynamic Church which seeks to continue its faithfulness in building God's kingdom'.[21] What are your comments? Is catechesis about exciting people or just communicating a certain amount of information?

- 'Stability and living the Christian faith as a member of the ecclesial community are basic requirements for catechists. They must mature as spiritual persons in the concrete tasks they perform, in such a way that the "first word" they speak is that of personal witness. To this must be added a professional competence, or the ability to sustain a journey with their brothers and sisters . . . In a word, the catechist of adults will be a sufficiently balanced human being, with the flexibility to adapt to different circumstances'.[22] How do you view this invitation and challenge of the ministry of catechesis?

Notes

1 CONVERTS TO CHRISTIANITY

1. For a more detailed exposition of the process of initiation see Thomas M. Finn, 'It Happened One Saturday Night: Ritual and Conversion in Augustine's North Africa', in Michael Warren (ed.), *Sourcebook for Modern Catechetics*, Volume 2 (Winona, Minnesota: Saint Mary's Press, Christian Brothers Publications, 1997).
2. Liam Kelly, *Sacraments Revisited* (Darton, Longman & Todd, 1998), p. 41.
3. 'It is significant testimony to the Church's obedience to the catechetical task in the early Middle Ages that catechetical texts like the Creed and the Lord's Prayer are almost invariably among the oldest surviving samples of writing in the newer European languages', M. McGrath, 'Basic Christian Education From the Decline of Catechesis to the Rise of Catechisms', in *A Faithful Church: Issues in the History of Catechesis* by Westerhoff and Edwards (eds.) (Wilton: Morehouse-Barlow, 1981).
4. Quoted by Gerard S. Sloyan, 'Religious Education: From Early Christianity to Medieval Times' in Michael Warren (ed.), *Sourcebook for Modern Catechetics*, p. 127.
5. ibid., p. 128.
6. ibid., p. 128.
7. ibid., p. 130.

2 FROM CATECHESIS TO CATECHISMS

1. Pierre Babin with Mercedes Iannone, *The New Era in Religious Communication* (Minneapolis: Fortress Press, 1991), pp. 23–4.
2. F. Thompsett, 'Godly Instruction in Reformation England: The Challenge of Religious Education in the Tudor Commonwealth' in Westerhoff and Edwards (eds.), *A Faithful Church: Issues in the History of Catechesis* (Wilton: Morehouse-Barlow, 1981), p. 179.
3. Quoted in Pierre Babin and Mercedes Iannone, *The New Era in Religious Communication*, p. 27. It is interesting to note that Luther expounds the virtues of memorization followed by explanation, while more than four

hundred years later the *General Directory for Catechesis* (1997) advocated that memorization should be preceded by explanation of texts.

4 ibid., p. 28.

5 Pope Pius V, *Catechism of the Council of Trent for Parish Priests* (Rockford, Illinois: Tan Books and Publishers, Inc., 1982), p. 3.

6 ibid., p. 4.

7 ibid., p. 4.

8 ibid., p. 7.

9 cf. Patrick M. Devitt, *A Brief History of Religious Education* (Dublin: Dominican Publications, 1992), p. 65.

10 Alain Peyrefitte, *Le mal francais* (Paris: Flammarion, 1977), pp. 162, 166–174.

11 Canon F. Drinkwater, 'On the making of catechisms', Downside Review, n. 256, Spring 1956, p. 130, quoted by Damien Lundy FSC in 'A vision for catechesis in the 1990s', in *The Candles Are Still Burning – Directions in Sacrament and Spirituality*, ed. Mary Grey, Andree Heaton, Danny Sullivan (London: Geoffrey Chapman, 1995), p. 45.

12 The influence of St Charles Borromeo can still be seen, since the schools run by the Confraternity were the forerunners of the many 'Sunday schools' operating today. The organisation itself had many ups and downs over the centuries but is still strong in many parts of the world. One of its most fervent supporters was Pope Pius X, who, in one of his first encyclicals, *On teaching Christian doctrine* (1905), decreed that the Confraternity should be canonically established in every parish.

13 Mary Charles Bryce, 'The Baltimore Catechism – Origin and Reception', in Michael Warren (ed.), *Sourcebook for Modern Catechetics* (Winona, Minnesota: Saint Mary's Press, 1983), p. 140.

14 R. Rummery, *Catechesis and Religious Education in a Pluralist Society* (Sydney: Dwyer, 1975), quoted in Patrick M. Devitt, *That You May Believe*, pp. 68–9.

15 cf. Michael Donnellan, 'Bishops and Uniformity in Religious Education: Vatican I to Vatican II' in *Sourcebook for Modern Catechetics*, p. 235.

16 ibid., p. 242.

17 Patrick M. Devitt, *That You May Believe*, p. 74.

18 Josef Jungmann, 'Theology and Kerygmatic Teaching', *Lumen Vitae* 5 (1950), 258–263.

19 Luis Erdozain, 'The Evolution of Catechetics' in Michael Warren (ed.), *Sourcebook for Modern Catechetics*, p. 90.

20 ibid., p. 92.

21 F. H. Drinkwater, *Educational Essays* (London, 1951), pp. 95–6, quoted in Josef Andreas Jungmann, *Handing on the Faith – A Manual of Catechetics* (Freiburg: Herder, 1955), p. 56.

22 Josef Andreas Jungmann, *Handing on the Faith*, p. 58.

23 Berard Marthaler, 'The Modern Catechetical Movement in Roman Cath-

olicism: Issues and Perspectives', in Michael Warren (ed.), *Sourcebook for Modern Catechetics*, p. 281.

24 *The Constitution on the Sacred Liturgy*, n. 64.

25 ibid., n. 65.

26 Such a statement was very much an endorsement of the educational principle, See–Judge–Act, espoused by the Belgian Joseph Cardinal-Leon Cardijn (1882–1967), founder of the Young Christian Workers Movement.

3   THE DECADE OF THE *DIRECTORIES*

1 Brother Gerard Rummery FSC, '1970–1980: The Decade of the Directories', in *Voice of the Hidden Waterfall, Essays on Religious Education* (Slough: St Paul Publications, 1980), pp. 17–18.

2 *A New Catechism, Catholic Faith for Adults* (London: Burns & Oates, New York: Herder & Herder, 1967), Foreword, p. v.

3 Cardinal Heenan, *Teaching the Faith, A Talk to Teachers and Parents* (London: Catholic Truth Society, 1972), p. 4.

4 *On Evangelization in the Modern World*, n. 4.

5 ibid., n. 18.

6 ibid., n. 4.

7 ibid., n. 41.

8 ibid., n. 76.

9 ibid., n. 29.

10 ibid., n. 44.

11 *Catechesis in our Time*, n. 1.

12 ibid., n. 6.

13 ibid., n. 6.

14 ibid., n. 15.

15 ibid., n. 18.

16 ibid., n. 21.

17 ibid., n. 22.

18 The Bishops' Message to the People of God (n. 18) had stated: 'Some [catechetical] methods insist on a doctrinal approach, some are more experiential; some emphasise anthropological aspects, some are more centred on dogma; some focus on political and temporal aspects, others stress spiritual formation. Any radical position will only be to the detriment of the preaching of the Gospel. A synthesis is made in a dialectic between the two'.

19 *Catechesis in our Time*, n. 52.

20 ibid., n. 53.

21 ibid., n. 55.

22 ibid., n. 55.

23 ibid., n. 59.

24 *On Evangelization in the Modern World*, n. 40.

[25] *Catechesis in our Time*, n. 63.

[26] ibid., n. 67.

4 R.C.I.A. – RITE OF CHRISTIAN INITIATION OF ADULTS

[1] Rev. William Bauman in the Introduction to *RCIA, A practical approach to christian initiation for adults* by Rosalie Curtin scl, Carl Koch fsc, Lillian Maguire scl, Jeanne Helen Stewart asc, and Terrence McGlennon fsc (Dubuque, Iowa: Wm. C. Brown Company Publishers, 1981), p. 2.

[2] *Constitution on the Sacred Liturgy*, n. 64.

[3] Rev. William Bauman in the Introduction to *RCIA, A practical approach to christian initiation for adults*, p. 2.

[4] *Rite of Christian Initiation of Adults*, n. 75, para. 2 (London: Geoffrey Chapman, 1987).

[5] ibid., n. 75 para. 3.

[6] ibid., n. 105.

[7] William R. Bruns, *Guiding Your Parish Through The Christian Initiation Process* (Cincinnati, Ohio: St Anthony Messenger Press, 1993), p. 135.

[8] *Rite of Christian Initiation of Adults*, n. 106.

[9] ibid., n. 126.

[10] ibid., nn. 234, 236.

[11] ibid., nn. 41, 42.

[12] ibid., n. 47.

[13] ibid., n. 106.

[14] William R. Bruns, *Guiding Your Parish Through The Christian Initiation Process*, p. 44.

[15] *Rite of Christian Initiation of Adults*, n. 128.

[16] ibid., n. 131.

[17] ibid., n. 16.

[18] *Adult Catechesis in the Christian Community*, n. 25 (Slough: St Paul Publications, 1990).

[19] ibid., n. 17.

[20] ibid., n. 28.

[21] ibid., n. 52

[22] ibid., n. 48.

[23] ibid., nn. 57–8.

[24] ibid., nn. 72–3.

[25] Anne Marie Mongoven op, 'Overview of the *Rite of Christian Initiation of Adults*' in *The Catechetical Documents – A Parish Resource* (Chicago: Liturgy Training Publications, 1996), p. 421.

[26] *Adult Catechesis in the Christian Community*, n. 32.

[27] ibid., n. 61.

[28] ibid., n. 73.

5   A NEW *CATECHISM* AND A NEW *DIRECTORY*

1   David McLoughlin, 'The treasure-house of faith', in *The Tablet*, 28 May 1994, p. 657.
2   B. J. Hilberath, quoted in Joseph Cardinal Ratzinger's *Gospel, Catechesis, Catechism* (San Francisco: Ignatius Press, 1997), p. 9.
3   *Catechesis in our Time*, n. 50.
4   For a fuller treatment of this see Berard L. Marthaler, 'The Ecclesial Context of the Catechism' in Berard L. Marthaler (ed.), *Introducing the Catechism of the Catholic Church* (London: SPCK, 1994), pp. 5–17. Marthaler notes that in preparation for the Extraordinary Synod Walter Kasper of the University of Tübingen wrote a paper for the German bishops in which he spoke of a 'crisis' or 'collapse' in catechetics.
5   ibid., p. 5.
6   *Guidelines for the Use of the Catechism of the Catholic Church*, p. 5.
7   *Catechism of the Catholic Church*, n. 23.
8   ibid., n. 24.
9   Dermot A. Lane, 'The Doctrine of Faith' in *Commentary on the Catechism of the Catholic Church*, ed. Michael J. Walsh (London: Geoffrey Chapman, 1994), p. 46.
10 *Catechism of the Catholic Church*, n. 1698.
11 ibid., n. 1075.
12 Joseph Cardinal Ratzinger, *Gospel, Catechesis, Catechism*, p. 18.
13 Berard L. Marthaler, *Introducing the Catechism of the Catholic Church*, p. 17.
14 *General Directory for Catechesis*, n. 120 (London: Catholic Truth Society, 1997).
15 ibid., n. 30.
16 ibid., n. 30.
17 ibid., n. 149.
18 ibid., n. 80, quoting *Catechesis in our Time*, n. 5.
19 ibid., n. 80, quoting *Catechesis in our Time*, n. 20c.
20 ibid., n. 67.
21 ibid., n. 87.
22 ibid., n. 153.
23 ibid., n. 59.
24 ibid., n. 39.
25 ibid., n. 110.
26 ibid., n. 109, quoting *On Evangelization in the Modern World*, n. 20.
27 Berard L. Marthaler in *The Living Light*, An Interdisciplinary Review of Catholic Religious Education, Catechesis, and Pastoral Ministry, Department of Education United States Catholic Conference, Washington DC, Winter 1997, p. 5.
28 *General Directory for Catechesis*, n. 66, quoting *Catechesis in our Time*, n. 22.
29 ibid., n. 156.

6 **SO WHAT ABOUT CATECHESIS TODAY?**

1 Apostolic Constitution *Fidei Depositum* on the publication of the *Catechism of the Catholic Church*, John Paul II, n. 3, contained in the *Catechism of the Catholic Church* (London: Geoffrey Chapman, 1994), pp. 5–6.
2 St Augustine, *Enchiridion ad Laurentium*, n. 6, written *c.* 421.
3 Dominic F. Ashkar, *Road to Emmaus – A New Model for Catechesis* (San Jose, CA: Resource Publications, Inc., 1993), p. 28.
4 Carroll Stuhlmueller CP, 'The Gospel According to Luke' in *The Jerome Biblical Commentary* (London: Geoffrey Chapman, 1968), Vol. II, p. 162.
5 Dominic F. Ashkar, *Road to Emmaus*, p. 77.
6 ibid., p. 90.
7 ibid., p. 95.
8 ibid., p. 105.
9 ibid., p. 113.
10 ibid., p. 46.
11 *General Directory for Catechesis*, n. 137.
12 ibid., n. 140.
13 Maureen Gallagher, *The Art of Catechesis* (New York/Mahwah, N.J.: Paulist Press, 1998), p. 17.
14 *Catechism of the Catholic Church*, n. 24.
15 *Directory on Children's Masses*, n. 2.
16 *General Directory for Catechesis*, n. 172.
17 ibid., n. 175.
18 ibid., n. 181.
19 ibid., n. 184.
20 ibid., n. 185.
21 ibid., n. 178.
22 ibid., n. 180.
23 ibid., n. 73.
24 'There is a close connection, and at the same time a clear distinction, between religious instruction and catechesis, or the handing on of the Gospel message. The close connection makes it possible for a school to remain a school and still integrate culture with the message of Christianity. The distinction comes from the fact that, unlike religious instruction, catechesis presupposes that the hearer is receiving the Christian message as a salvific reality. Moreover, catechesis takes place within a community living out its faith at a level of space and time not available to a school: a whole lifetime', Congregation for Catholic Education, *The Religious Dimension of Education in a Catholic School*, n. 68 (London: Catholic Truth Society, 1988).
25 Jim Gallagher SDB, *Guidelines* (London: Collins Liturgical Publications, 1986), p. 27.
26 *Directory on Children's Masses*, n. 2.

[27] Adult Catechesis in the Christian Community, n. 32.

[28] cf. *General Directory for Catechesis*, nn. 94–6.

[29] ibid., n. 240.

[30] Archbishop Weakland's Foreword, in *The Art of Catechesis* by Maureen Gallagher, p. 2.

[31] *General Directory for Catechesis*, n. 240.

[32] ibid., n. 128.

[33] Bishop Sylvester Ryan of Monterey, California, in *Origins* (CNS Documentary Service) 1 May 1997, p. 735.

[34] *Catechism of the Catholic Church*, n. 2725.

[35] *General Directory for Catechesis*, n. 237.

[36] Bernadette Tourangeau, 'Adaptation to the Audience's Situation and Context of Catechesis', in *The Living Light*, Winter 1997, Volume 34, Number 2 (Department of Education, United States Catholic Conference, Washington, DC), p. 51.

7   SOME PASTORAL CONCERNS

[1] *Adult Catechesis in the Christian Community*, n. 61.

[2] *Catechesis in our Time*, n. 67.

[3] *General Directory for Catechesis*, n. 158.

[4] ibid., n. 234.

[5] ibid., n. 235.

[6] ibid., n. 235.

[7] *The Interpretation of the Bible in the Church*, Part IV, Section C, n. 3 (Quebec: Éditions Paulines, 1994).

[8] *General Directory for Catechesis*, n. 241b.

[9] ibid., n. 242.

[10] ibid., n. 244.

[11] *Catechism of the Catholic Church*, n. 426.

[12] Cardinal John Henry Newman, *The Development of Christian Doctrine*, 1845.

[13] *Pastoral Constitution on the Church in the Modern World*, n. 11.

[14] *General Directory for Catechesis*, n. 117.

[15] ibid., n. 205.

[16] cf. ibid., n. 149.

[17] *General Catechetical Directory*, n. 46.

[18] Tony Ashcroft, *Becoming a Catechist* (Great Wakering, Essex: McCrimmons, 1988), p. 18.

[19] St Augustine, *Instruction* 1.18.19, quoted in Garry Wills, *Saint Augustine* (London: Wiedenfeld & Nicolson, 1999), p. 70.

[20] John Paul II, *Christifideles Laici, Post-Synodal Apostolic Exhortation on the Vocation and the Mission of the Lay Faithful in the Church and in the World* (London: Catholic Truth Society, 1988), n. 17.

²¹ Maureen Gallagher, *The Art of Catechesis*, p. 14.
²² *Adult Catechesis in the Christian Community*, nn. 72, 73.

Bibliography

Ashcroft, Tony, *Becoming a Catechist* (Great Wakering, Essex: McCrimmons, 1988)

Ashkar, Dominic F., *Come to the Wedding Feast – An Eight-Session Course for Training Catechists* (San Jose, California: Resource Publications, Inc., 1996)

Road to Emmaus – A New Model for Catechesis (San Jose, California: Resource Publications, Inc., 1993)

Babin, Pierre, with Iannone, Mercedes, *The New Era in Religious Communication* (Minneapolis: Fortress Press, 1991)

Bishops' Committee for Catechesis and Adult Christian Education, Bishops' Conference of England and Wales, *A Gift Destined to Grow – an invitation to study the General Directory for Catechesis* (Chelmsford: Rejoice Publications, 1999)

Bruns, William R., *Guiding Your Parish Through the Christian Initiation Process: A Handbook for Leaders* (Cincinnati, Ohio: St Anthony Messenger Press, 1993)

Catechetical Documents – A Parish Resource (Chicago: Liturgy Training Publications, 1996)

Devitt, Patrick M., *That You May Believe – A Brief History of Religious Education* (Dublin: Dominican Publications, 1992)

Fogarty, Philip, SJ, *Why don't they believe us? Handing on the Faith in a Changing Society* (Dublin: The Columba Press, 1993)

Gallagher, Maureen, *The Art of Catechesis – What You Need to Be, Know and Do* (New York/Mahwah, N.J.: Paulist Press, 1998)

Grey, Mary, Heaton, Andree, and Sullivan, Danny (eds.), *The Candles are Still Burning – Directions in Sacrament and Spirituality, Essays in Honour of Christiane Brusselmans* (London: Geoffrey Chapman, 1995)

Jamison, Christopher, OSB, Lundy, Damian, FSC, Poole, Louisa, SSL, *'To live is to change' A way of reading Vatican II* (Chelmsford, Essex: Rejoice Publications, 1995)

Jungmann, Josef Andreas, *Handing on the Faith – A Manual of Catechetics* (Freiburg: Herder, 1959)

Kelly, Francis D., *The Mystery We Proclaim – Catechesis At The Third Millen-*

nium (Huntington, Indiana: Our Sunday Visitor Publishing Division, Our Sunday Visitor, Inc., 1993)

Manternach, Janaan, and Pfeifer, Carl J., *Creative Catechist – A comprehensive, illustrated guide for training religion teachers* (Connecticut: Twenty-third Publications, Mystic, 1995)

McCarty, Jim, *The Confident Catechist* (Dubuque, Iowa: Brown Publishing, ROA Media, 1990)

Marthaler, Berard L. (ed.), *Introducing the Catechism of the Catholic Church* (London: SPCK, 1994)

Nichols, Kevin, *Cornerstone, Guidelines for Religious Education/1* (Slough: St Paul Publications, 1978)

Voice of the Hidden Waterfall, Essays on Religious Education (Slough: St Paul Publications, 1980)

Nichols, Kevin and Cummins, John, *Into his Fullness, Guidelines for Religious Education/2* (Slough: St Paul Publications, 1980)

Olszewski, Daryl, *Everyday Theology for Catholic Adults* (Dublin: The Columba Press, 1989)

Pfeifer, Carl J. and Manternach, Janaan, *How to be a Better Catechist* (Kansas City, MO: Sheed & Ward, 1989)

Questions Catechists Ask & Answers That Really Work (Kansas City, MO: Sheed & Ward, 1993)

Ratzinger, Joseph Cardinal, *Gospel – Catechesis – Catechism, Sidelights on the Catechism of the Catholic Church* (San Francisco: Ignatius Press, 1997)

Study Group of the Bishops' Conference of England and Wales, *Signposts and Homecomings, The Educative Task of the Catholic Community, A Report to the Bishops of England & Wales* (Slough: St Paul Publications, 1981)

Warren, Michael, *Faith, Culture, and the Worshipping Community – Shaping the Practice of the Local Church* (Washington, DC: The Pastoral Press, 1993)

(ed.), *Source Book for Modern Catechetics* (Winona, Minnesota: Saint Mary's Press, Christian Brothers Publications, 1983)

(ed.), *Source Book for Modern Catechetics*, Volume 2 (Winona, Minnesota: Saint Mary's Press, Christian Brothers Publications, 1997)